THE SAVVY STUDENT'S GUIDE TO COLLEGE EDUCATION

By TheBestSchools.org
with Patrick O'Connor

Foreword by Dr. Ben Carson

Education Axis
Bellevue, WA 98004
www.educationaxis.com

Copyright © 2016 by Education Axis. All rights reserved. No part of this book may be reproduced, stored in a retrieval system, or transmitted, in any form or by any means, electronic, mechanical, photocopying, recording, or otherwise, without the permission of Education Axis.

Designed and typeset by Education Axis
Printed in the United States of America

Library of Congress Control Number: 2016946777

ISBN: 0-9815204-5-6
ISBN: 978-0-9815204-5-2

Contents

Foreword by Dr. Ben Carson	i
Introduction	1
Selecting the Right College for You	3
Selecting a College Major	13
The College Application Process	23
Writing Effective College Application Essays	35
Researching Scholarship Opportunities	47
Financing a College Education	57
Benefits and Pitfalls of Student Loans	67
Career Prospects of Different Majors	77
Career Trends: Where the Jobs Are	87
Writing an Effective Résumé	97
Giving a Successful Interview	109
Your First Day on the Job	121

FOREWORD

My name is Dr. Ben Carson and I am the co-founder of The Carson Scholars Fund, a non-profit organization with two educational missions:

1. the Carson Scholars Program, which honors students in grades 4–11 who excel academically and are dedicated to serving their communities;
2. the Ben Carson Reading Project, which has established reading rooms at schools throughout America to create a literacy enriched environment for children to develop their reading skills.

The Carson Scholars Fund commissioned TheBestSchools.org to produce this guide to college education as a means of assisting our scholars with their educational endeavors after graduating from high school.

The Savvy Students Guide to College Education was thus intended, in the first place, to help students and supporters associated with the Carson Scholars Fund. However, we soon realized that the advice and information in this guide were relevant not only to our scholars, but to all students seeking higher education through college.

The information in this guide is a must-read for all students, parents and educators who are involved in, or soon-to-be involved in, the college decision-making process. I hope that you find this information helpful as you begin to plan for the next step in your future.

–Dr. Ben Carson

INTRODUCTION

You decide you want to go camping. You have a vision of the perfect weekend. There will be hiking, fishing, meals cooked over an open flame, and S'mores. Oh man, S'mores! You can see yourself coming back to school on Monday refreshed and feeling great about yourself and nature. Friday comes and drags by but then finally the awaited weekend has come!

But, your camping weekend is an unmitigated disaster! How did this happen? Everything was going to be perfect, just the way you imagined it. Well, the weekend flopped because no planning or preparation went into the trip. There was no research into the best campsite, no careful selection of which gear worked best for this time of year in your area, nothing.

Too many times this is exactly the way many prospective students approach some of the most important decisions they will ever make – their college selection and their choice of study. While it's perfectly normal (and acceptable) to spend long spring afternoons your senior year daydreaming of walking across the stage Magna Cum Laude at Harvard, that dream has very little chance of becoming a reality unless some serious planning and preparation has already been going on for several years. There's so much to consider.

What is the right school for me? Should I start at a two-year school or go directly to a four-year school? Will I get in? Which major should I choose? How am I going to pay for this? You are by no means the first person to face these difficult questions. After years of dealing with these kinds of questions, The Carson Scholars Fund commissioned TheBestSchools.org to come up with a guide for their scholars. But realizing that this guide holds information of interest to all high school graduates, TheBestSchools.org decided to make it available to everyone.

This twelve-chapter guide addresses everything from beginning the search for your ideal college your freshman year of high school (Yes! It should start that early) to your first day of classes as a new college student, to preparing for a job and onward to tips for your first day in a job. Don't know how to write an effective admission essay? There are great tips for that. Worried about paying back student loans until you're in your seventies? The Savvy Student's Guide will give you the information you need to borrow responsibly as well as tips for researching scholarship opportunities. Wondering if you'll be able to get a job with that basket weaving major that sounds so cool? Maybe check out Chapter 9: Career Trends so you can know where the jobs are before you invest your hard work, time, and money.

A successful college experience takes planning, and planning for something you've never done before is difficult. The Savvy Student's Guide to College Education is here to help.

About the Author:

Patrick O'Connor began helping college-bound students and families make wise higher education choices in 1984. An award-winning college counselor, O'Connor has served students from all walks of life. In addition to writing for www.collegeisyours.com and having works appear in High School Counselor Week, The Washington Post, Diverse: Issues in Higher Education, O'Connor teaches Political Science at Oakland Community College and is Director of College Counseling at The Roeper School, both in Metropolitan Detroit.

O'Connor has served as president of the Michigan Association for College Admission Counseling, and the National Association for College Admission Counseling. O'Connor also sits on the board of directors of the Michigan College Access Network, and on the credentialing commission for the American Institute of Certified Educational Planners. Additionally, he has received the Margaret Addis Service to NACAC Award, the William Gramenz Award (for outstanding contributions to college counseling), and Outstanding Faculty Award from Oakland Community College,. He holds five college degrees, including a Ph.D. in Education Administration.

Selecting the Right College for You

The Big Picture

Many students are surprised at how easy it is to choose between the thousands of colleges out there. But once you have a clear understanding of who you are, what you like, and how you best learn, picking a college becomes a pretty easy and fun thing to do. Learning about yourself is something you've always done, and that's the key to a successful ninth grade, where you ramp up and fine tune your self-knowledge by learning to be a good student, participating in clubs and activities, and learning how to help others. You keep building these skills throughout high school, while you begin to visit local colleges in tenth grade, so you can get a better understanding of the different kinds of colleges that are out there. In eleventh grade, you'll visit more campuses and meet college admissions officers that visit your school or home town, all while continuing to grow as a student and as a person. This gets you ready to build your first college list in the spring of eleventh grade, a list that will change and grow, but serve as a place to begin to develop the college options you'll choose from in spring of the senior year.

You would think picking a great college would be a pretty easy thing to do – and in many ways, you're right. While there are over 3600 colleges in the United States alone, most people will apply to no more than six, after visiting no more than two dozen, and doing online research on less than 50.

What is it that gets students so excited about these colleges, and makes it so easy to focus on only less than two percent of the many college choices out there? The same thing that makes it easy to pick out your favorite foods at the grocery store, the few online videos you watch over and over again, and the clothes you buy out of all of the options you have at the mall – you learn to know what you like. Starting with a strong understanding of who you are, what you need from a college, and where you'd like to go in life, picking a college can be as fun as choosing what new songs to download, and just as easy.

The Start of Your College Search, and Ninth Grade

Most students think the college search begins some time in tenth or eleventh grade, when a parent, teacher, or school counselor sits you down in front of a computer or a very thick college guide and asks you to pick out the names of some colleges you'd like to investigate. That's certainly an important step in the college selection process, but since your college choice is based on your interests, talents, and needs, you're really preparing for your college search since birth, as you learn about what you like to do, subjects you like to study, places where you like to hang out, and careers you might pursue. In many ways, looking at the menu of college choices is like looking at the menu of a restaurant where you're eating for the first time. No matter how big the menu is, it would be a little intimidating, if this were the first time you'd ever eaten – but a lifetime of experience leads you to make great choices.

A big part of the life experience that shapes your college choices is your time at school – elementary school, middle school, and high school. College is a great experience both in and out of the classroom, but the biggest part of that experience involves challenging yourself with new ideas. Every day you spend in school of any kind gives you a chance to shape the way you take on new ideas, whether it's learning Algebra in high school, or learning about what makes a flower grow in first grade. Over time, your ability to take on new ideas and work with them becomes the basis of your study habits, your grades, your hobbies, and the way you look at life – and all of those things are part of the college application process.

Since choosing a college is really just another way to show the world what matters to you, you can begin your preparation for college at any time. College readiness means you have the classroom skills, study habits, and decision-making tools necessary to make the most out of the learning experiences of college, and you become college ready with every class you take in school.

College readiness consists of three big parts, and the first big part is study skills. By figuring out how you best study, you are learning more about how you learn. That's different for everyone, so it's more than

OK if your friend knows they can only study in a quiet room at a desk, while you can study on the bus, or one friend uses flash cards to study, while you need to study by reading everything out of the book. When it comes to study skills, there's no such thing as one best way to study. There are better ways for you to study, and learning about those is a big part of school. Your teachers can help you figure out the best way for you to study.

The second big part of college readiness lies with extracurricular activities. The sports teams, clubs, and hobbies you develop may just seem to be fun to you, and they should be. But these activities also help you learn more about yourself and the world around you. They also help you develop essential skills that will really pay off in college and in life. Skills like getting up early in the morning for practice, tracking down the answer to that hard question for Model UN, or perfecting that tricky move on the dance floor require the ability to keep at a task even when it's tough, to think about others as well as yourself, and to put in a lot of time to something that matters to you. All of these skills offer big payoffs, and the biggest one is knowing more about yourself and what you can do, all while you're having a good time.

The third part of college readiness is learning to give back to others. It doesn't always seem like it, but many of the opportunities you have in the world are the result of people who do things to help you, even when there's nothing in it for them. The teacher who meets with you after school doesn't get paid any more to do that; they just care about what you learn. The referee who works the basketball games at the community center is getting paid next to nothing; they're really there because they want you to have a chance to play. The person who picks up the trash on Saturday mornings on the road you take to schools wants everyone to have a cleaner neighborhood, including you. Community service may seem like one more thing your high school might require so you can graduate, or something you do just to help out other people. But as you keep doing things for others, you start to see how important that work is, and how it changes the way you see the world, all for the better.

As a student, you're always studying, playing, and helping others, so it should come as no surprise that you should keep doing those things in ninth grade. What surprises most people is that, to be college ready, that's really all you have to do in ninth grade. If you really want to, you can start researching colleges then, and it's always a good idea to visit a college campus when you can. But the best college choice begins with knowing who you are, what you like to study, and what you can give to the world – and that's what college readiness is all about. So if you really want to be college ready, spend ninth grade doing what you've always done – making the most out of every opportunity.

Tenth Grade

You'll be working on college readiness throughout high school, so every year, you will continue to use and explore the study skills that work best for you; you'll keep pursuing the teams, activities, and hobbies that mean something to you, and you'll look for opportunities to help others. No matter how well you did these things in ninth grade, tenth grade gives you the chance to do more of them in different ways. Be sure to make the most of this new opportunity.

Tenth grade is also the time many students start to learn about the different kinds of colleges that are out there. Chances are you've heard about different colleges before, and even been on campus to watch their teams play or go to a concert. All of those experiences are important as you think about what you want to do after high school, and tenth grade is an important time to understand more about each of those choices.

There's a good chance your school counselor will introduce you to different kinds of colleges in tenth grade, either through some kind of classroom presentation, or through an online exercise where they give you guided virtual tours of colleges. These are important experiences, but the best way to learn about colleges is to get on some college campuses and experience them in person. If your high school doesn't arrange college visits for you, work with your parents and your friends to visit campuses on days when school is out. Most colleges that offer tours let you sign up for them online, while other colleges don't offer tours, but will let you come and walk around.

In visiting college campuses in tenth grade, you want to get a feel for how colleges are similar, and how they're different. To do this, you want to make sure you're visiting different kinds of colleges – and most students don't have to travel too far to do that. A quick online search of "Colleges within 100 Miles from Here" should give you a wide number of campuses to look at, all within an easy drive of home. As you choose, make sure you're investigating as many different kinds of colleges as possible, including:

Four-year residential colleges
These are colleges where students work towards a Bachelor's Degree, while living on campus or in student housing near campus.

Four-year commuter colleges
These are colleges where students work towards a Bachelor's Degree, while living at either their own home or their parent's home. Most four-year colleges offer students the choice of being residential or commuter colleges, but some require students to live on campus for at least the first year.

Community colleges
Community colleges, or colleges where students are working on a certificate, Associate's Degree, or classes that will allow them to transfer to a four-year college. Some community colleges offer housing options, but most are largely commuter schools.

It's a good idea to visit at least one of each kind of college in tenth grade, and it's even better to visit at least two of each kind. This may mean some students have to travel farther than 100 miles from home; if that's the case, try and design your college visits so you can see one college in the morning, and one in the afternoon. It's usually best to only see two colleges in one day, so you can remember the details of your visit.

What should you do once you're on campus? Take the tour, for sure. These tours are designed to introduce you to the most important parts of the college, and to answer any specific questions you might have about the college. To make the most out of the tour, take about 30 minutes to look at the college's website. Make sure to look at the list of majors they offer. It is more than OK if you don't know what you want to study, but it's good to know what they offer. Also, take a look at their student life, or activities section, so you can know what it's like to be on campus when you're not in class. And be sure to sign up for the tour!

Once you're on campus, listen closely to the tour guide. This will likely be a student from the college, and while they've been given a script of information to share with you, you can learn a lot from how they tell you the information, the jokes they make, and the way they answer any questions people have. It's great if you bring some questions along to ask the tour guide, especially if you want to know about specific classes, programs, or activities the college offers.

As you take the tour, and especially once it's over, try to get a feel for the atmosphere at the school. How is it the same as your high school? How is it different? Are the students friendly – are they too friendly? Do they like to study and socialize as much as you do, or are they a little more serious about school – or less serious?

If you can visit a class, do it. It's best to visit a freshman class, and you only have to stay for 15 or 20 minutes, but classes are a big part of the college experience, so it's good to see what they're all about. The same is true for looking at where students live, and where they eat. Finally, see if you can find a place on campus where the students hang out. Stay there for at least 20 minutes as well, and just people watch. Once you're done people watching, ask yourself: Do I feel comfortable here? What do I like about this college? Is there something missing that would make me feel more comfortable here? It's good if you know what's missing, but even if you don't, it's important to know that you're looking for something else in a college that may not be here.

As soon as your visit is done, write down what you think about the college, good and bad. Some students take notes on their phone; some will use a notebook, and others will put their thoughts in an online organizer that's offered through their high school. No matter where you put your final notes, make sure you write these ideas down right away – and write them down before you talk with your friends or parents about what they think of the college. Their opinions are important, but it's always best to start with a clear idea of what you think.

Summer programs

Tenth grade is also a good time to think about experiencing college life through a summer program. Since many colleges don't offer classes in the summer, some will offer special programs to high school students, so they can take a course they don't have time for during the regular school year, try out a class where they can explore a career, or take a course their high school doesn't offer. Many of these classes are taught by college professors, and some are available at little to no cost. Registration for these programs usually starts in January or February.[1]

Eleventh Grade

Students are continuing to take the most challenging classes they can in junior year, all while developing stronger and more advanced study skills. Extracurriculars continue to be a big part of your life, as you take on roles of leadership in clubs and teams you've been a part of for a long time (something colleges like to see) and as you explore new interests. The same is true with community service, as the number of hours you're contributing now begins to total the hundreds, and you have the chance to assume leadership positions in these volunteer activities.

Your exploration of colleges also continues in eleventh grade, but it begins to take on a more specific focus. You don't have to know what college you want to attend at this point, but your tenth grade college visits and the research you're doing on colleges on web sites are probably pointing you to a number of colleges that have a great deal in common.[2]

You can build on the success of your tenth grade college visits in three important ways. First, continue to visit campuses you've researched online. These visits are very much like the visits you took in tenth grade, except this time, you're not just going to see what makes one kind of college different from another – you're going to see if this is a school you'd like to attend. Your eleventh grade search could lead you to touring colleges farther away from home, and that's great, if you're comfortable with the idea of being somewhere new for school. Qualities like the size of the college, where it's located, what programs it offers, and how much it costs are all a part of choosing a school, and every student has their own likes and dislikes. Junior year is the time to discover what yours are, and campus tours will do that.

Since some colleges are just too far away to visit, colleges will often come to meet you. Many college admission officers will schedule

---

[1] A great list of summer programs for high school students can be found at http://summerprogramfinder.com/.

[2] Two great websites to explore while doing college searches can be found at https://bigfuture.collegeboard.org/college-search, and https://www.cappex.com/

time to come to your high school and talk with you about their school, while other colleges will hold these same kinds of meetings at an area hotel. This is a great way to get to know a college before deciding to spend the time and money to visit campus. Be sure to bring your questions to these meetings, and don't be afraid to ask them, even if there are lots of other students around. Asking good questions is one way to get noticed by a college, and that can be an important part of the application process.[3]

This list of questions is also good to use when attending a college fair, where dozens of colleges send representatives to talk with students and parents. Usually held in the fall or spring at a local high school, these fairs are open to students throughout the area, and give you the chance to get to know a lot about many colleges, all at the same time. Just like a college visit, it's best to do a little online research about the colleges before you attend the fair, since there are so many colleges to choose from once you're there. At the same time, it can be fun and beneficial just to pick one or two colleges at the fair you've never heard of, and start talking with the admissions representative.

Making Your First College List

By spring of junior year, it's a good idea to begin to put together a list of colleges you'd like to apply to. The application process itself won't start until summer or fall, but it's a good idea to develop a list and share it with your parents and your school counselor. This is the team that will help you apply to college, and what they know about you and your college interests can help them support your choices.

Just like each student's college choice is different, the college list for every student is also different. Students looking at certificate programs or community colleges may have only one or two colleges on their list, based on the programs the student is interested in, and the location of the colleges. Other students may be looking for four-year colleges that are so popular, they only admit a very small percentage of the students who apply. In this case, students will want to include a number of colleges where they would be happy to attend, since there is

---

[3]Don't know what to ask? Take a look at http://www.nacacnet.org/college-fairs/students-parents/Documents/CollegeFairChecklist.pdf for some ideas.

no guarantee these highly selective colleges will admit even the most successful students.

For students thinking about four-year colleges, a good starter college list usually includes:
- One or two colleges in the student's home state. Many students start their college search with an interest in going far away for college, but those plans often change by the end of senior year. Adding these schools keeps that option open.
- One or two colleges where the student's grade point average (GPA) and ACT or SAT test scores are the same, or higher, than the average GPA and test score for students admitted at that college, and where the college admits 20 percent or more of the students who apply.
- One or two colleges where the student and their family can afford to pay for college without having to take out too many loans. Just what "too many" means is different from student to student, but every student has to make sure they aren't just applying to schools that will require them to take on a lot of debt.

All of the research, visits, and things you know about yourself should come together in a way that you've found schools that fit well with your interests, needs, and abilities. This "fit" is that feeling you get on a campus tour when you just know this is a place where you'd love to live and learn after high school, and it is one of the keys to a strong college choice.

While every college you apply to should give you a good feel for fit, this beginning list of 3-6 colleges should also give you a wide menu of options to choose from when you have to decide what college to attend, a decision you make in the spring of your senior year. That's important, since what you're looking for in a college could change between the time you make your first list in junior year, and time you actually have to choose a college, once you're done applying.

More Resources

For a list of additional resources visit:
http://www.thebestschools.org/savvy-students/chapter-resources/

SELECTING A COLLEGE MAJOR

The Big Picture

One of the most exciting parts of applying to college is thinking about what the major focus of your studies will be once you get there. In choosing a major, students will want to get a good understanding of all the possible majors that are out there, since most high schools don't offer classes in every single major. After doing that research, students may want to think about what they'd like to do as a job or career, since many jobs require students to complete some kind of training in a specific major. By completing interest inventories and aptitude tests, students will get a sense of the careers they may like, and what careers they have special talents in. Once these are complete, students will want to visit college campuses to get a better understanding of what it's like to study that major on a regular basis.

Many students who begin college with one major will change to another major – in fact, most students will change their major at least three times. These changes can be made for a number of reasons, but with each change, it is important that the student understand how many of the classes they've already completed will apply to their new major, and how many additional classes they may have to take. Students who start college without a major may want to consider attending a liberal arts college, where programs are designed for students to investigate different majors in the first two years. Other students who are undecided in their major may want to design their own major, an option that is available at most colleges. Attending other colleges as an Undecided major is always an option, but students will want to work closely with an adviser once they do choose a major, so they can understand how many of their classes will transfer into that major, and know what classes to take to complete their degree on time.

"*So, what's your major?*" When you're heading for college, it seems like everyone asks you this, along with "*Where are you going to college?*" It's also the question you'll be asked the most once you get to college, as your fellow freshmen try to get to know you better.

Since you hear this question so often, it's understandable that you want to have an answer – and a really good one. But how do you know what you want to major in? What if you change your mind? What if you don't know what major is right for you – can you still go to college?

These are all great questions, and they all have more than one answer. Let's take a look.

Researching Majors

Check the College Catalog

The first step towards doing a really strong search for majors is realizing there are lots of majors out there you don't know about. Too many high school students use the subjects offered in high school as their only guide to choosing a major, when colleges offer so many more academic regions to explore. Consider this partial list of majors that aren't covered in most high schools:

- Advertising
- Anthropology
- Archaeology
- Astronomy
- Data Analysis
- Forestry
- Histology
- Historiography
- Neuroscience
- Supply Chain Management

And more are being created every year.[1] If you really want to get a good idea of what's out there, spend about 15 minutes looking at the list of majors of any large university, but the majors list of your local state university will be just as interesting. Once your 15 minutes is up, write down the names of every major you remember. You've just seen

---

[1] The majority of this list of majors was pulled from Michigan State University at https://admissions.msu.edu/academics/majors_list.asp?Level=UN&Sort=Major.

a lot of majors, but some are staying with you, and there's a reason for that. Pick a couple, and do a Google search of them, to see what that field is all about, and whether it might be of interest to you.

Consider Your Career Options

Another way to create a list of possible majors is to think about the careers you might be interested in. Getting some ideas about jobs that might interest you is as easy as taking an interest inventory, which doesn't take long, and can offer some great ideas on careers you might like, and might not like.

There are quite a few interest inventories out there for you to use. If you're in high school, there's a very good chance your school will give you an interest inventory of some kind in ninth or tenth grade.[2] These results give you some ideas about possible careers, but remember: these aren't the careers you have to pursue. They're just some possibilities.

It's important to remember that these interest inventories don't cover all careers, and the results they give are based on the kinds of activities you like to do. Some of the careers you find may require some level of skill, or aptitude, that make it more challenging for you. Aptitude tests also exist online, but the results of these tests aren't always reliable. Many aptitude tests ask you to rate your own abilities, which means the results are based on how you see yourself – they don't actually measure your skills. For example, you may see your physical strength as very low, compared to your friends – but if your friends are all football players, you might actually be very strong compared to most people.

If you're looking for an aptitude test that actually measures your skills, it's tough to beat the Armed Services Vocational Aptitude Battery, or ASVAB.[3] The ASVAB is often given by high schools, or by a local armed services recruiter, and since the test is required of everyone applying to join the military, it's very likely you will be getting a lot of phone calls and email from recruiters once you take the

---

[2]If your school doesn't offer one, take a look at these two assessment websites: http://www.assessment.com or https://myroad.collegeboard.com/myroad/navigator.jsp.

[3]The ASVAB is located at http://official-asvab.com/, but if you are looking for a nice beginning, self-evaluating aptitude test, take a look at http://www.whatcareerisrightforme.com/.

test. You can certainly take other aptitude tests, but they will likely require a fee. Check with your school counselor.

Once you have a sense of the kind of careers that might interest you, it's time to look at the Occupational Outlook Handbook.[4] The OOH gives you an outline of the kinds of education experience you need to have, including what you may need to study in college.

This is a very important piece of information, since many people assume that a career has just one or two majors associated with it, when there are usually many majors associated with a career. This is especially true for students interested in becoming doctors and lawyers, where they think they have to be a pre-med major or a pre-law major. Where that used to be true, most medical schools and law schools are now interested in students from all kinds of backgrounds. It will still be important to study organic chemistry and anatomy before applying to medical school, but many programs will now accept medical students who majored in Engineering, Business, History, and even Music. The same is true for law schools, where they're looking for good thinkers and good writers – and what major doesn't help you do both of these things?

Seeing the major in action

Once you develop a list of possible majors, it's time to take a campus tour. In addition to talking to people in the admissions office, you'll want to make sure you have time to sit in on a class in the major you're interested in, or talk with the academic adviser in the department where your major is offered. Conversations with advisers are a great way to get the latest information about the major, including new career fields where the major is popular, and new classes being offered in the major. Academic advisers are often the experts in connecting majors with jobs, so they are good people to know!

Changing a Major

So you've investigated the options, done some research on majors, looked into some of the career options related to the major, and decided on your major.

---

[4] Located at http://www.bls.gov/ooh/

And then it happens. You're in the middle of an economics class you're taking as a Business major, and it makes no sense to you. You're about to dissect your first frog as a pre-Med major, and you faint at the sight of blood. You talk to a visiting professor as a Music major, and find out they really don't make any money. What now?

It's important to know that people change majors all the time. There aren't any formal studies on this issue, but the general rule in college is that most people will change their major at least three times once they're in college – and that doesn't even include the major you choose before you start. Some will find the subject too easy, others will find it too hard, and many will find it uninteresting, but there are other reasons why people change majors that they have control over. Keep these in mind as you research possible majors.

You don't want to think about the subject all the time

Many people begin studying a subject they like, only to discover they don't really want to talk about it every single day of the week. Just like people who will watch only one baseball game a year, there's a limit to how interested some people are in Biology or Accounting – but they don't really know that until they've studied it past their comfort zone.

It isn't what you thought it was

It isn't unusual for college students to change their major after an internship, or job shadowing experience, where they came to understand just what it means to work in this field on a full-time basis. Sometimes, this is due to having to think about the subject all of the time; sometimes, it's about the kinds of people you work with in the field; sometimes, it's just not as exciting as you thought it would be.

You have to study a related field you really don't like

Most Business majors can relate to this, since they have to study Economics for at least a year to earn their Business degree, and Economics can really drive people crazy. It's also true with Political Science majors who have to take History, and Journalism majors who have to memorize parts of speech. Writing about exciting things sounds great, but committing gerunds to memory is a different story.

The career path in that major changes
We saw this ten years ago, when the demand for lawyers dried up overnight, and lots of students who were History majors decided they needed to find something else to study.

You find something else you'd rather study
Not all students who change their majors are running away from something they don't like – sometimes, they're running towards something they like more. It's easy for this to happen, especially in a large college, where students may discover by literally walking into it, by taking a wrong turn in a hallway, or taking a shortcut to a class.

A new major is invented
This also happens more often than people realize. Colleges are developing new majors to meet research and employment demands, creating niche majors that can give students a huge advantage when it's time to look for a job – as long as it's in that specialty field.

Whatever the reason you change your major in college, students will want to keep a close eye on the graduation requirements of the new degree. If the student is changing their major to a new area that's closely related to the field they are currently studying – say, from Chemistry to Biology – there's a good chance the first few courses they have to take in both of those fields will be similar, if not identical. In this case, changing majors won't affect how long it will take the student to complete their degree, since the credits in one major will transfer to another.

On the other hand, students making a big change in majors – say, from Chemistry to Business – may find that many of the classes they took, even in the first year of college, aren't required for a Business degree. If that's the case, it's going to take longer to earn a degree in your new field, which will take more time, and more money.

Students thinking about changing their major will want to spend some time with the adviser in the new field they want to study, to find out just how many of the classes they've already completed will transfer, and how much longer they will need to be in college to complete their degree. Asking your current adviser these questions won't do you any good, since they won't be as familiar with the graduation requirements of your new major. This is especially true if you are transferring in or out of a specialty program like Art, Engineering, or Music. Most of the first year classes in these fields usually apply only to that major, so any change means you will likely be starting college over.

It's also important to think about when you will change majors. Since most students change their majors several times in the first two years of college, many colleges make sure students take classes in their first and second years that will apply to all majors. These core courses are in fields like English, Math, Social Science, and the Humanities, and taking them allows the student to change majors without losing as many credits.

Students changing majors after two years in college will probably be looking at needing to take at least one additional year of college, depending on the major they have, and the major they are going into. Even if the fields are closely related, most majors want college juniors to take courses that focus in on that subject, which means the courses would only count as elective credit in another major. Since elective credits are pretty easy to find, juniors changing majors will end up with far more elective credits than they need, which means more years of college are likely. That isn't a bad thing, especially if you like learning, but it is important to understand that if you're changing majors later in your college career.

Not Having a Major

There are an incredible number of high school students who don't know what they want to study in college. After completing an interest inventory and looking through college categories, they either find too many majors they'd like to study, or they have no idea what they'd like to look at in college on an in-depth basis.

If that sounds remarkable, it really shouldn't. An incredible number of adults are working in a job that has nothing to do with what they majored in while they were in college. It may have been an unexpected job opening where they needed someone at the last minute; it may be a career opportunity they were introduced to by a friend who knew them well, and didn't really care what they had studied in college; it may be a brand new career path that doesn't have a traditional college major associated with it. No matter what the case may be, the major-career connection isn't always clear cut, especially as people get older.

What's really remarkable is the way many high school students who don't have a major in mind just make one up. When a relative asks them, "What's your major?" they really don't want to say "I don't know", since they worry the relative might be worried by that response – or, worse yet, criticize the student. As a result, the student responds by saying "Astrophysics" in the hopes that answer will keep the relative happy. (Just to let you know, it usually doesn't. They'll ask what astrophysics is, and when it's clear you can't tell them, they'll get nervous anyway.)

If you're thinking about college and you have no idea what you want to study, that's actually pretty great – as long as you choose the right college. Many colleges are designed to make sure students take core courses in the first two years that will count towards every degree the college offers, as well as some survey courses that give students some idea of what it would be like to major in a particular field. Known as liberal arts colleges, these four-year schools are usually attended by students who want to keep their options open as far as majors go – so much so that, in many cases, most students graduating from liberal arts colleges go on to graduate school, now that they know what they want to study, to earn an advanced degree.

Of course, not everyone who attends a liberal arts college is looking at six (or more) years of college. There are a number of business leaders who believe that liberal arts students make the best employees in business, since the business world requires creativity, flexibility, and innovation, skills that are a key part of the liberal arts experience. To these employers, there's nothing better than to have a brand-new college graduate as part of your team, as your company trains them in the essentials of business, making the most of the critical skills their new employee has learned in college.

Since liberal arts colleges aren't for every student who is undecided about their major, you'll want to also look at the options many colleges have for self-directed majors, or degree programs where the student designs their own major. The most famous of these colleges is Hampshire College in Massachusetts, where every student is required to design their own major. This may sound like fun, and it is – but it's also serious business. Students work closely with advisers to develop a plan of study that outlines every class they'll take, and the student must present this plan to a board of review for approval. Students completing their programs are rightfully proud of their work, not only because they designed their own program, but because Hampshire has very high academic standards. If you graduate with a Hampshire degree, it's clear you have an impressive set of skills.

Hampshire may be the most famous "do it yourself" school, but it isn't the only one. While they don't advertise it, most colleges allow some students to design their own major, using the same framework as Hampshire. This includes some of the largest public institutions in the United States – it's just that, unlike Hampshire, you have to ask about the program.

Other students will attend other colleges as well, and use the college's resources to select a major. In this case, students need to keep in mind the same rules as students who change majors – make sure you take core courses in your first year, and be prepared to sacrifice some credits if you start a major in junior year. College degrees are designed to address a specific set of skills, so even going from Undecided to, say Business, requires the student to complete a set of courses they might not have had access to. Again, the key is working with an adviser, and working with them early.

Getting ready for college is an exciting time because college offers so many opportunities for students to try out new things, learn new ideas, and learn more about themselves and their relationship to parts of the world that are completely new to them. Many high school students may have a good idea what they want to focus in on in their college studies, but a good number of them that do will change that focus many times in college. As students think about college, it's good to keep a major in mind, but don't feel like you have to have a major before you go to college, since many college like it when you have no idea what you want to study, since that leaves your future wide open.

More Resources

For a list of additional resources visit:
http://www.thebestschools.org/savvy-students/chapter-resources/

THE COLLEGE APPLICATION PROCESS

The Big Picture

Once senior year arrives, it's time for you to build a plan to complete your college applications. Using what you've learned as juniors by researching colleges and visiting college campuses, your first list of colleges will probably be between 6-8 schools, with each school on the list meeting a special need of either being close to home; a college where your chances of admission are above average; a college that's affordable, or a college you just plain love.

After completing the list, you'll want to think about the plusses and minuses of applying to any of your colleges under an Early Action, Early Action Restricted, or Early Decision, program. The deadline dates of each application will help you decide which application to work on first – but no matter when the application is due, you want to order official copies of test scores in late August or September, to make sure they arrive on time at the colleges that require them.

Once you've built your list and know the deadlines, it's time to complete the applications, including any essays and interviews that may be required by some colleges. The key to success with these parts of the application is to keep the approach conversational, since the goal of both is for the college to get to know you as a person, and as someone with more to offer than just good grades and test scores.

If you haven't already done so in spring of your junior year, the start of senior year is also the time to ask for letters of recommendation from your teachers, making sure to give them ample time to write a quality letter. One of the biggest advantages you can give a teacher letter of recommendation is to waive your right to see the letter.

Once an application is submitted, keep a close eye on your e-mail account. You may not use e-mail very much, but most colleges will acknowledge receipt of an application by e-mail, and e-mail you to ask for more information if they need it. Be sure to look in your junk mail folder, since a great deal of college e-mail ends up there.

Colleges will notify you with a decision to admit, reject, defer, or waitlist your application. With the exception of a rejection, each decision requires you to take additional steps in the admission process. In some cases, you can appeal a rejection, but this is rare.

With strong campus visits in the junior year, and a clear plan for completing applications in the fall of the senior year, you can make the most of the college application process, and still enjoy homecoming, prom, graduation, and all the other events that make senior year great – all while getting ready to begin a new chapter of your life in college.

In the chapter on selecting the right college, we talked about the importance of fit – finding colleges that have the right mix of programs and atmosphere that will challenge, support, and excite you. By looking at college websites and taking campus tours in your junior year, you start to understand what makes one college different from another (size, location, school spirit), and what makes some colleges seem like a better fit for your goals and interests.

Knowing what you're looking for in a college makes the application process that much easier. By taking a little time to get organized in the fall of senior year, you'll have plenty of time to prepare strong applications colleges will take seriously, while visiting even more college campuses, and enjoying the activities and traditions that make senior year awesome. This will make senior year enjoyable and productive, giving you all the time you need to find colleges that are perfect for you, without worrying too much.

Before You Apply – Building a College List

You'll want to begin your senior year with a list of six to eight colleges you're interested in. This list may change throughout senior year, but it's important to have a good starting list based on the qualities you're looking for in a college. This will give you a way to evaluate any new colleges you may hear about or visit in your senior year, and that can help you decide if a new college should be added to your list, or even replace another college on your list.

Six to eight colleges may seem like quite a few, but it's easy to build your list if you create it two colleges at a time. The first two colleges that go on your list are colleges you'd like to attend that are in the state where you live, or close enough to where you live that it would be easy to come home if you needed to.

In the fall of senior year, it might seem like the last thing you want to do is go to college somewhere close to home, but it's important to keep that option open, in case an unexpected family situation requires you to start your college career nearby. In addition, the cost of attending a public college or university as a state resident often reduces or eliminates the need to take out student loans (more about that later), and many state colleges offer honors or residential programs that will offer a quality learning experience with small class sizes and direct access to professors. It's important to keep this option open during senior year, and that's why these two colleges are a must.

The next colleges that go on your list are two colleges you'd like to attend where your GPA and test scores are above the average GPA and test score at that college. In addition, these colleges have to admit more than 20 percent of all students who apply. Your chances of admission are very good at these colleges, and it increases the chances you may qualify for a merit scholarship – money you don't have to pay back once college is over. In looking for colleges that meet this requirement, students can once again look for colleges that offer strong honors or residential programs for top students, but these colleges can be anywhere in the country, or in the world.

The next two are colleges you'd like to attend that require the least amount of borrowing or financial aid. Cost can be a very big factor in deciding which college to attend, and you can't always tell how much aid you will receive from every college. By looking at a college's cost of attendance and their net price calculator (both on the college's website), you can get a good idea which ones will cost less, and leave you with the least amount of debt once you graduate. These go on your list.

The last two colleges are schools you would just love to attend. These may be schools that are so popular, you can't be sure you'd be admitted, or they may be schools where your grades and test scores are below those of the average admitted student, but you really like them. Since you never really know about admission and affordability until you apply, add these colleges to your list – and if there are more than two, add those as well, as long as you know you'll have time to submit a strong application to all of them. (And what about that college you really like, but can't explain why? Put it on the list.)

As you put your list together, you may find a college that fits in more than one category – for example, there may be a school in your state that has a very low tuition where your grades and test scores are above their averages. If you're interested in that school, put it on the list. That may mean you end up with only four or five colleges on your list, but since they all fill at least one important role, your list is perfect.

Other students run into the opposite problem, where they have so many schools they simply love, they end up with a list of more than six or eight – and sometimes, their list is twice that long. If your college list has 10 or more schools, it's time to think carefully about the time and the money involved in submitting so many college applications. Given everything else you have to do senior year, will you really have time to put together a strong application for each of your colleges? Can you afford the extra $300-$500 you might need in application fees?

Finally, if you apply to, say, six dream colleges, will you be ready to accept the colleges' decisions if they all say no – and if all of those rejections come on the same day? It's more than OK to be brave and take chances; just remember to make a back-up plan in case your dream school doesn't come through for you.

Applying Early

Once you have your starter list put together, it's time to decide if you want to apply to any of your colleges through a program where you get your admissions decision earlier than the spring of your senior year. Early programs give students more time to make their final college choice, and for many students, that lets them enjoy more of their senior year, knowing their future plans are all in place.

There are three kinds of early programs:

Early Action
Early Action programs allow you to apply by a specific date (usually in November or December) and hear back from the college in about 8-10 weeks, well before the typical response date in late March or early April. If you're admitted as an Early Action (or EA) student, you still have until May 1 to decide which college to attend, and it doesn't have to be the college that admitted you through an Early Action program. The advantage here is that you hear back from the college earlier than usual, but you still have plenty of time to make a final college choice. Many colleges offer Early Action as an option, and you can apply EA to as many colleges as you'd like.

Early Action Restricted

Early Action Restricted (EAR) offers the same advantages of Early Action, but if you apply through a Restricted program, that's the only early program where you can submit an application. Colleges that offer EAR want to make sure you've really thought about your decision to apply early, and that you know enough about the college to feel that it would be a very good fit for you.

The rules of EAR can be a little hard to follow. Some private colleges that offer EAR will allow you to apply to other public colleges as an Early Action candidate, while other colleges place different limits on your Early Action applications that are unique to their college. The website of the college will explain what limits apply to their EAR application programs – but it isn't a bad idea to talk to a counselor or call the college if the rules aren't clear.

Early Decision

Early Decision programs also have early deadlines, but in this case, if you're admitted through an Early Decision program, you must attend that college. Once a college notifies you that you have been admitted as an Early Decision (or ED) applicant, and they meet your financial aid needs, you must withdraw your applications from all of your other colleges. You don't get to find out if other colleges admitted you, or how much financial aid they would have given you. Once your ED college says yes to you, and if they meet your demonstrated financial need, your college application process is over.

If ED sounds like an option for only a few students, you're right. There aren't many students who start their senior year knowing what one college they absolutely want to go to more than any other college, who are willing to promise to stop looking at other colleges if their first choice college takes them as an ED student. Because ED students are so interested in one college, ED colleges usually admit a larger percentage of ED applicants than they do students who apply through the regular admission process.

Since ED makes your chances of admission greater, it may sound like something you want to do – but remember, if the college admits you ED, you have to go there. If this college is one of many you like, ED may not be the option for you. It's kind of like buying new clothes. You may love the first thing you see, but do you love it so much, you're willing to buy it before seeing anything else?

Many colleges also admit a larger percentage of their applicants through an Early Action program, but being admitted as an EA applicant doesn't mean you have to attend that college. Since EA programs allow students to hear back from the college early, while still having until May 1st to make a final college choice, more students apply to EA programs than ED programs. Some colleges offer both EA and ED, while others don't offer either. Be sure to check the application descriptions and deadlines for all of your schools.

Ordering Your List

Now that your initial college list is complete, it's time to decide which application to complete first. To do that, visit the website of each college, and enter the following information in the table below:

College Application Tracker

COLLEGE NAME	Application Date EA, ED, or Regular?	# of Required Essays	Test Scores Required	Teacher Letters? How Many? From Whom?

Using this table as your guide, begin work on the application that is due first. You might think you should start on the application with the most essays, but if that application isn't due until late January or December, you'll have more time to work on those – and you don't want to miss the deadline of an easier application.

In completing this table, make sure you know which of your colleges have a rolling admissions program. These colleges include most public colleges, and they often have a very late application deadline (like February 15 or March 30), but rolling admissions means they make decisions on applications in the order they are submitted. This usually means that students applying in October or November will hear back in December – and if there are more students admitted then, that will make it harder for students to be admitted who apply later in the year. This is even true for very large colleges that have rolling admissions deadlines – the longer you wait to apply, the harder it can be to get admitted. As a general rule, students should apply to rolling admissions colleges no later than October 15. There may be some exceptions to that rule, so check with your school counselor.

Ordering Test Scores

No matter when an application is due, you'll want to have official results of your ACT and SAT scores sent in August or September to the colleges that require them. These orders can sometimes take up to a month to be delivered to the colleges, and no college that requires test scores will review an application without a copy of the results sent directly from the testing company. It doesn't matter if your application comes after your test scores arrive; colleges will hold on to your test scores until June of your senior year.

If you've already had your scores sent when you took the test, you don't have to send them again. In addition, some colleges will require you to send the results of every ACT and SAT test you've taken in 11th or 12th grade, while other colleges will let you decide which test scores to send. Check the admissions requirements of each college, and also see if the college will *superscore* your test results, by taking the best scores from different test dates to give you the highest possible test result. For example: you scored 24 on the Math section and 27 on the Science section of the ACT in April, but in June, you scored 26 on Math and 23 in Science. A college that superscores the ACT will take the 27 from the April Science test, and the 26 from the June Math test. If a college does that, be sure to make sure you're sending all of your best scores.

If you aren't sure what test scores to send, it's better to send the results of every test you've taken. No college I know of penalizes students for low scores if they've sent in higher scores – and if you forget to send in all of your results to a college that requires them, they may deny you admission just because you didn't give them everything they asked for. You've worked too hard for that to happen – so, when in doubt, send all scores.

Kinds of Applications and Their Contents

There are three kinds of college applications:

Basic Application
A basic application asks you to supply some personal information (name, home address, date of birth), some information about your high school (name, address, expected date of graduation, GPA, senior year schedule), and some information about your college plans (intended major, will they live on campus, full-time or part-time study).

Enhanced Application
An enhanced application asks for the same information, and requires you to submit either an essay or teacher letters of recommendation.

Holistic Application
A holistic application asks for the same information as a basic application, as well as one or more student essays, and one or more teacher letters of recommendation. Some holistic applications will also require an interview.

We'll talk more about the do's and don'ts of essays and interviews in another chapter. For now, it's safe to say you should just be yourself – and give some thought to covering up your tattoos at a first interview.

Teacher Letters of Recommendation

There are three keys to getting effective teacher letters of recommendation. Since the main reason you're going to college is to learn, colleges want to find out what it's like to work with you as a student in an academic class. That's why letters of recommendation need to come from a teacher who has worked with you in your junior or senior year, and has taught you in an academic area (English, Math, Science, Social Science, Language).

If you're going to major in art or music, the college may want a letter from your teacher in that area as well, but you will still most likely have to submit a letter from an academic teacher, too. If a coach or a boss wants to tell the college about what it's like to work with you, it's usually OK to send one extra letter, but only one – check with your college.

Since writing a good letter of recommendation takes time, it's important to give the teacher advanced notice. Many students will ask teachers in the spring of junior year. This doesn't mean the teacher will write the letter then, but it does give them a chance to schedule a time to write the letter and still get it into the college on time. If you have to ask in the fall, make sure you give the teacher at least three weeks to write their letter and submit it to the college.

Finally, a good letter of recommendation is written about you, but it isn't written to you. The Family Educational Rights and Privacy Act (FERPA) allows you to see your letters of recommendation after you've been admitted to the college, but most colleges ask you if you want to waive that right when you first apply.

It's wise to waive your right to see your letters. Some teachers feel a little nervous about writing a letter of recommendation you will eventually see, and that can affect the quality of the letter. In addition, some colleges wonder why you don't trust the teacher you've asked to write your letter of recommendation, and that can affect your admission. It's best to pick a teacher you trust, and waive your right.

After You Apply

Most college applications are online, so the first thing you want to do once you apply is make sure the college has received your application. Colleges will usually send you an e-mail within two or three days after you apply to let you know they've received your application. This e-mail will sometimes end up in your junk mail folder, so check it often, since this is also where your e-mail notice of acceptance could end up! If you don't hear from the college a week after you've applied, call the office of admission to make sure they've received it. E-mail and phone calls may seem a little old school, but that's how most colleges communicate with students, so make sure you're comfortable using both.

Once you know the application has been received, all you can really do is wait to hear from the college, while keeping your grades up and enjoying your final year in high school. The only time you should contact the college before you hear back from them is if they ask you for additional information, or if you have a change in your senior year schedule. Some colleges will also ask you to let them know when you are suspended or disciplined at school after you apply. If they ask about this, you need to tell them, but you should first discuss how to do this with your counselor. (And do I really have to remind you it's better not to get suspended at all?)

Kinds of Decisions

A college can make one of five decisions on your application:

Admission

Admission means they have accepted you as a student, provided you graduate from high school and continue to earn the same grades you've been receiving. Admission often means you'll have to submit an enrollment deposit, something you can do any time until May 1st.

If you plan on living on campus, you may have to make a housing deposit earlier than that, and either way, you'll probably have to attend some kind of orientation program. Read all of your admission information closely, and make a list of all of the information and deposits you need to submit to the college. If it's going to be hard on your family to find money for the deposits, call the college and ask what your options are; they may be able to waive the deposits.

Provisional Admission

Provisional admission means the college has accepted you, provided you meet some additional requirements. This usually means you're allowed to enroll, but you have to maintain a certain GPA in your first year of study. It may also mean you have to participate in required study skills or tutoring programs – or in some cases, start going to college in the summer. If you're offered provisional admission, make sure you read and understand the terms of admission.

Rejection

Rejection means the college has not accepted you for enrollment. In many cases, rejection decisions are made because the college simply has too many qualified applicants, and not enough room to admit all of them. In other cases, the college has reviewed your application, and has determined that you would not be a successful student at that college.

Rejection isn't easy to take, but very often, this has nothing to do with you – it's all about the college not being big enough to take in every student they like. This is why it's important to build a good-sized list in the start of senior year. When it comes to music, you may like some bands more than others, but everyone likes more than one or two bands, and for different reasons. This is why your playlist is diverse, and it's why your college list should be, too.

If you receive a rejection notice, and you aren't sure why you were rejected, you can usually contact the college for more information, but it would be a good idea to talk with your counselor first. Very few colleges offer an appeals process to reconsider an application, but if you realize there's something you didn't tell the college that might affect your admission status, they may reconsider your application.

Deferral

Deferral means the college needs more information before they can make a final decision on your application. Deferrals are usually given to students who apply Early Action or Early Decision, and the college feels they need to know more about you. In many cases, the college will ask for your current grades in your classes, and perhaps a new set of test scores. In other cases, the college will let you send in the additional information they've requested, as well as any other information you'd like them to consider.

If a college lets you submit additional information, be sure to take them up on the offer. Write a brief letter of 3-4 paragraphs that includes updates on what you've been doing since you submitted your application. This would include any new grades, but it would also include your work in clubs, sports, and activities, any awards you may have earned, or anything else you would like to share with them. This is also an opportunity to send another letter of recommendation to the college, if you have a letter you didn't already send, or if there is another teacher who could write a strong letter on short notice.

Once you submit this additional material, wait another 5 weeks or so. If you haven't heard back from the college, send another brief note that states your interest in the college, and gives them any additional updates. (And don't send them selfies with you wearing gear from that college. That usually comes across as cheesy.)

Waitlisted

Waitlisted means the college will be happy to admit you as a student, as soon as they have room for you. Since not every student who is offered admission accepts the offer, this can create room for the college to move students off the waitlist, and accept them for admission.

If a college waitlists you, they will want to know if you would like to remain on the waitlist and still be considered for admission. If you do, this may also be a time to send them additional information about your accomplishments since the time you applied, and an additional letter of recommendation. Some colleges will accept this material, and others won't – read your waitlisted letter to see what your college allows you to submit.

If you decide to stay on the waitlist, it's important to put in an enrollment deposit at *another college by May 1*. Most colleges will review their waitlisted students in early May, and if you aren't offered admission at that point, you want to make sure you have a college to attend – that's why putting in a deposit at another college before May 1st is so important. If you are offered admission after May 1 as a waitlisted student at another college, just notify the college where you've put in a deposit that you will be attending another college. You can ask for your deposit back, but don't be surprised if the college denies your request.

Many students think applying to college is a complicated process. With a little advanced planning, and a clear understanding of what you're looking for in a college, you should be able to work on one application a weekend, staring in September, and be finished applying to colleges by Thanksgiving – and a little work always beats a lot of stress.

More Resources

For a list of additional resources visit:
http://www.thebestschools.org/savvy-students/chapter-resources/

WRITING EFFECTIVE COLLEGE APPLICATION ESSAYS

The Big Picture

Many students don't think the college essay matters all that much in the college application, but since this is the only time students can "talk" to a college, the essay proves to be very important. Since colleges are reading the essays to get a sense of the student's "voice", you'll want to write a personal essay that shows them how you think, how you feel, and what matters to you in the world. The "Why Us" essay asks students to explain what they see in the college that makes it a special place to them, and how they plan on making the most of what the college has to offer. In answering both of these kinds of essays, the student will want to make sure they communicate in an honest way that completely answers the question, and that they do so in their own words. Students will also want to make sure they aren't being too personal in their responses, and that they select an editor for their essays who is willing to support the student's efforts to write their own best essay, and nothing more.

In many ways, the essay is the most important part of the college application. Think about it: the grades you've earned in your high school classes tell part of the story of who you've been, and so do your test scores. But where do the colleges get to find out who you are now, and learn more about what matters to you, what you think about, and what you'd like to do in the future? All of those answers can be part of a strong college essay, where sharing the story of your life can make all the difference between bringing your application to life, and being just another applicant with a bunch of numbers.

But most students don't see it that way. They view the college essay as just one more part of the application, another item on the college checklist they have to take care of. Besides, writing is hard. It takes a long time to put together a book report, or a research paper – and that essay on what I did on my summer vacation? Please!

It's easy to see that most of the writing students do is hard – but a lot of it is pretty easy, too. Think about all the writing you do that has nothing to do with school. Texting your friends, posting captions with your pictures online, talking about who did what at a recent concert, or what someone wore to the music awards show. It isn't hard to write then – in fact, most students love to write then. You put an opinion out there, someone responds, you post an answer, someone else jumps in the conversation, and suddenly, there's a real exchange of ideas going on. Nothing stuffy or boring, but the real you, talking about real ideas.

If it's done well, that's exactly what a good college essay does – inspires ideas. If they could, the college you're applying to would have you come to campus, take a tour, talk with the admissions officer for an hour or so, get some lunch, talk a little bit more with the admissions officer, grab some swag at the bookstore, and then head home. If they did that, they'd really know who you are, and what matters to you. But if they did that with every applicant, they'd need 20 years to decide who gets admitted.

Since they can't do that, they ask for your side of those conversations in writing – and just like a face-to-face conversation or a really good text discussion, the quality of the conversation in the college essay is all up to you. Instead of seeing this as one more part of the application, think of it as the best chance you're going to get to show them who you are, and your goal is to get them so focused in your world, that they'll look up at the end of the essay and wonder where you went, because they'll feel like you've been talking with them. You can do that with a good post to social media, so you can also do it with a good college essay. It isn't quite the same thing (no LOLs in a college essay), but the tone is very similar.

Kinds of College Essays: The Personal Statement

There are three different kinds of college essays, and the personal statement is the one most students are familiar with. Personal statements give the student an idea, or prompt, and ask the student to write about it. These prompts can be very detailed, like this one from The Common Application that's used by over 500 colleges:[1]

---

[1] See http://tinyurl.com/px7gg72. 2/25/2106

> Some students have a background, identity, interest or talent that is so meaningful they believe their application would be incomplete without it. If this sounds like you, then please share your story.

In the world of college applications, this is like your best friend texting you and asking, "What's up?" It isn't like a math problem, where there's just one answer, and it isn't like an English quiz, where they ask about just one part of the book. Here, you get to pick a part of your life to share with the college, and what it means to you. Where the story goes, and how you get there, is pretty much up to you.

To be honest, this is where most students blow it. Rather than see this as a chance to tell their story, they think they have to give a speech, or write a book report, which makes the tone of the essay very stiff and boring. Worse, some students think they don't have anything important to say. Since they haven't cured cancer, or won six Grammys, they feel like the college doesn't really want to hear their story. It's almost like the student is thinking, "They don't really care about me."

But here's the thing – they do care about you, or they wouldn't be asking the question – and if you had already cured cancer or won six Grammys, you wouldn't be going to college anyway! Think about the student who wrote about taking a plane ride. He didn't save anybody's life, or have to land the plane all by himself without radar – it was just a plane ride. But who he ran into on the plane, and how he interacted with them, created such a great personal statement, he was not only admitted to an Ivy League college, but got a handwritten note from the admissions officer, saying this was the best essay he'd read in two years.

This essay was about something lots of people do, but that wasn't what made it special. It was special because of the way the student told the story, showing what happened, and what it means to the student now that the experience is over. That's an important part of a good essay – show them, don't tell them. Consider the beginning of this essay, where a student talks about their experience on the track team:

> One of the most important parts of my ninth grade year was when I ran track. I was a freshman at the time, running the 400, and I was taking Algebra I, History, Earth Science, French I, and American Literature.

If you aren't bored reading this already, you should be. First, the student's already told us they are in the ninth grade, so we know they're a freshman. Second, the student's schedule is already on their grade report, or transcript. Does it really have anything to do with the story?

Most important, the tone isn't really bringing us into the story – and it needs to. The goal of a good personal statement brings the reader to you, not you to the reader. Something like this:

> They ran out of space when they built our high school, so the football field and the track were built on the edge of a swamp. That made for an inspiring spring track season in ninth grade, when the humidity was so high it made 400 yards on asphalt feel like slogging through the Sahara with an empty Aquafina bottle.

This essay puts the reader right on the track with the student. It still shows the student is running the 400, and still shows the student is in ninth grade, but it brings the reader right into the student's world. It's like the difference between this picture:

And this picture:

Both show you a track, but one gives you the feeling of the track. In personal statements, feeling is important.

That's important to keep in mind at the end of a personal statement. Now that you've told your story, the college wants to know what the story means to you, and why it's important – you could write about all kinds of stories, so why did you write about this one?

Again, you want to avoid sounding like a narrator, so this approach isn't quite what we're looking for:

> Looking back, I can see how much I grew as a person thanks to that track season. My GPA went up, I participated in several track camps over the summer, and I won the league championship the next year.

This is OK, but it's really more of a list than a description of what the experience meant to them. In addition, the college can already see the list of camps and awards in another part of the application. It's better to use the essay to share new ideas – like this:

> I taped the laces from my track shoes inside my locker at the end of freshman season. I replaced them with the league medal I won the next year, and replaced that with the medal I won junior year. If I learned anything from the heat of the swamp, it's knowing how to make the most out of each challenge, and to keep finding new ones. It's the only way you grow.

The end of this personal statement is a powerful glimpse of how the student sees the world, and that's a key part of a successful essay.

The "Why Us?" Question

Another essay topic colleges use is the "Why Us" question, where they want to know why you're applying to their college. There are thousands of college choices out there, and tools like The Common Application make it possible to apply to dozens of schools by completing just one application. Colleges want to make it easy for students to apply, but they also want to know the student is serious about applying. That's why they ask the "Why Us" question.

Take a look at this "Why Us" question from the University of Chicago:

> How does the University of Chicago, as you know it now, satisfy your desire for a particular kind of learning, community, and future? Please address with some specificity your own wishes and how they relate to UChicago.

This is a pretty typical "Why Us" question, and it has three parts:

What do you know about us?

A strong answer has to show the college you've taken a close look at what they have to offer. This is more than liking their location, their football team, or a few of their most popular majors. It means you've looked past the first few pages of their website, or did more than just take the standard tour when you visited campus. It's great if you want to go to a college to study Biology, but what does the college offer that makes you want to study Biology there? A special research program? A professor or two who are highly recommended by a friend? If it's the atmosphere of the college, what makes that school special? Student activities? The way the students interact with the teachers? The more details you know about the college, the better the chances you'll pick one that meets your needs.

What does college mean to you?

For many students, college is the first time they have a choice about where to go to school. That means it's important to think about what you're looking for in a college, and what you'd like to get out of the experience. All colleges offer classes and degrees, and most let you study in another country. What are you hoping to get out of those classes? Do you have some idea what you'd like to do once you're out of college? Are you a "hands-on" learner, looking for a chance to work closely with professors? Do you do better with large classes? Colleges want to know what you're looking for, so they can make sure they're offering what you need to make sure college is a happy, successful experience for you.

How well does our college meet your goals?

Once you show the college what you know about what they have to offer and what you're looking for, you have to show them how the two fit together. This may seem obvious, but it's an important connection many students overlook – and colleges want to know what you see in making that connection. Consider this answer to the University of Chicago question:

> The University of Chicago is located in one of the richest, most diverse urban areas in the United States. Relying on its strong history of scholarly excellence, UChicago places high demands on its students, and expects as much from its students outside the classroom as it does within.

This is a very nice summary of the college – but where does that leave the student? There's no connection here between personal goals and how the college can help meet the student's needs – and the essay is asking the student to answer that very question.

Then, there's this approach:

> That hot, humid spring on the freshman track team taught me a lot about setting new goals, and the importance of looking far and wide for answers that can help me grow. As I begin my career in Social Work, UChicago's history of success teaching students how to help others, and the rich diversity of the city of Chicago, provides the wide array of resources I'm used to working with, and making the most of. When it comes to moving new ideas forward, UChicago and I have a lot in common.

This is a great answer for three reasons. First, it starts with the student talking about them. Most students don't answer a "Why Us" question this way, but they should, since the question basically asks the student to tell the college what it has to offer the student – and the only way to know that is for the student to start by saying, "Here's who I am."

Second, this answer has the right balance of fact and feeling. The student did enough research on The University of Chicago to learn about its Social Work program; they combined this with the student's feelings about the importance of setting new goals, and put together a strong conclusion.

Finally, this answer is great because it draws on parts of another essay. In this case, the student used the track story from the first essay to bring home a point in the second essay. Creating this kind of bridge, or theme, across essays is something very few students to, and it's something colleges look for. This allows the student to create one larger story with the answers from two smaller essays, with an impressive result.

Application Essay Do's

Once you're finished with your essays, use this checklist to make sure you've followed these important rules:

Answer the question

If the college asks you to name someone who's inspired you, and they still don't know who that is once they read your essay, that's one reason for them to consider not admitting you. It's more than OK to be creative with your answers; just make sure your response addresses what's been asked.

Give more than a Yes or No answer

Some essay prompts may be written in a way where it would be easy to just agree or disagree. Not only is that the easy way out; it's also not a very interesting answer. If someone asked you in person if you're worried about global warming, you wouldn't just say Yes or No. Since the essay is really a conversation on paper, you want to give more of an answer here, too.

Include a mix of head and heart in your answer

Some prompts might also suggest they only want to know what you think about an issue, or what you feel about an issue. In almost every case, a good college essay includes both. "The wide array of studies supporting the idea of global warming requires us to study the issue more closely. I want my children to be able to study and come to love the wide variety of nature as much as I do." It isn't enough to talk about a feeling; tie it to a fact you've seriously thought about, and you're off to a good start.

Begin with an explanation, rather than an answer

Our student in the example didn't start his essay with "I joined the ninth grade track team." Instead, the author started with a description, drawing the reader in right away, while still letting them know where they were, and what they were doing. Let the reader jump into the story.

Show them to someone else to read

The person you choose should have a good understanding of grammar and you. While this usually is an English teacher, someone who doesn't know you won't be able to tell if the essay "sounds" like the way you talk and express yourself, and that's pretty important. If your grammar expert doesn't really know you, show it to two people, but no more.

Copy and paste the entire answer, and check to make sure you do
Since most college applications are online, students will write their essays on one computer program, then paste them into the online application. That works, as long as the entire essay makes it onto the application. Make sure it does, by reading the entire essay; and watch out for times when sentences in the middle of the essay have disappeared (it sounds weird, but it happens!)

Proofread!
Spell check is a great thing, but "I think night is my best time to study" doesn't mean the same thing as "I thin knight is my best time to study" – but spell check thinks both sentences are just fine. Do this proofreading once the essay is on the application.

Application Essay Don'ts

There are also a few things you want to avoid in your essays – here's the list.

Don't try and figure out what the "right" answer is
If the admissions office asks you to describe a place where you feel comfortable, they're not hoping you'll answer with "the library" or "the classroom." If you really do feel comfortable there, that's the answer for you – but if it's in the pool or at your aunt's house, those answers will work just as well, as long as you can show them why.

Don't write on a topic that's used a lot
Having just said that there is no such thing as a "right" answer, it's also important to know that some answers get used a great deal, and that can make it harder to write an essay on that topic that will get noticed. Many essays are written about being on a sports team. If that's only one example in the essay of how you've learned a lesson in life, you're probably OK; if it's the only example, you're running a big risk. If sports means a lot to you, be sure to expand your focus in your essays.

Sports can also cause problems with the "Why Us" question. Any part of your answer that talks about your lifelong desire to be in the student section rooting on the Eagles or Knights or – well, you get the idea – is usually seen as being a little shallow, even if the college has a strong sports program. Focus more on the other parts of being a student and a member of the community, and keep the sports references to one, if that.

Don't address an overly personal topic

Just like you don't have to have won a Nobel prize to write a great essay, you don't have to write about something extremely personal in an essay that asks you to describe a time you overcame adversity. One admissions officer tells students to think carefully before writing an essay about any of the 4 Ds – Drugs, Dating, Divorce, or Death – and to that, I would add a fifth D – Depression. This isn't to say the colleges don't care about these things; it's just that the goal of the essay is to show what you've learned about these challenges, and how you've moved on from them. Genuinely big challenges can take time to get over, and if you try and write about your experience too soon, the message you're trying to get across may suffer. If the topic for your essay involves something this personal, be sure to talk about it thoroughly with your counselor; it might be better for them to mention in their letter, freeing you up to write about something else.

Don't use another college's name in the essay

It's never a good thing when an essay sent to the University of Michigan ends with "And that's why I hope you'll give me a chance to be a student at Michigan State." It's more than OK to use parts of some essays to answer questions from different college applications, as long as the essay still answers the question – but changing the names of the colleges is a must.

Don't start being funny

The number of students who decide to begin their careers as comedians with their college essay is almost amazing as the number of students who get denied admission because their "funny" essays just aren't that funny. It's important to keep growing as a student, but the college essay shouldn't be the place to launch your practice as a poet, rapper, or comic. Rely on the voices you've used with confidence as a student and as a person, and lead from your strengths. Essays should show you, but they should show the best of you.

Don't let someone else write the essay for you

Some students – and, unfortunately, their parents – are convinced colleges don't know the difference between an essay that's written by a high school senior and one that's been "heavily edited" by a tutor, a student already in college, the applicant's parents, or someone on the internet who does this for a living. The truth is, the colleges can pick this up in a minute – and no, I'm not going to tell you how. Doing this violates the statement of integrity you sign when you apply, and it can serve as the reason to remove you from the college at any time if you end up going there. That's too much to risk; write your own essays, and use your editors lightly.

More Resources

For a list of additional resources visit:
http://www.thebestschools.org/savvy-students/chapter-resources/

Researching Scholarship Opportunities

The Big Picture

College scholarships continue to be one of the most important parts of the college application process, especially since a scholarship can make the difference in helping make any student's college dreams come true. When looking for scholarships, it's important to remember there are other kinds of funds that are also available to help pay for college – scholarships are money for college that's given based on a particular talent the student has. Scholarships break into two categories – the kind offered by companies and organizations, and the kind offered by colleges. It's harder to be selected for a nationally-known private scholarship than it is to receive one offered by a local group or by a college, but there are some ways to increase your chances – and part of that has to do with the student's interest in writing more essays for scholarships, on top of the essays they've already written for college. Some scholarships require students to prepare an audition or portfolio rather than an essay, while athletic scholarships have their own special requirements that are constantly changing. No matter what kind of scholarship the student receives, it's important to know the conditions the student is committing to when they agree to take the scholarship, and to understand how long the scholarship lasts.

There's something pretty great about going to college, but there's something even better about going to college on a scholarship. Whether it's based on the hard work you've done in the classroom, the talent you've made the most of as an athlete or artist, or just because somebody believes in you and your plans for the future, the feeling you get when someone appreciates what you're doing, and gives you a chance to do even more at college.

Since everyone likes to be recognized, and everyone likes something that's free, it isn't always easy to find scholarships for college, especially since more students are going to college than ever before.

But if you know where to look and how to apply, you can make the most of a scholarship search by building it around your interests and needs – and by looking in places where other people don't.

What is a Scholarship?

There are all kinds of resources out there to help students pay for college. In this chapter, we're going to focus on scholarships, or money for college that is given to a student based on a demonstrated talent. This talent can really be just about anything – strong work as a student, impressive performance as a dancer, being a good athlete, or even being a great yo-yo artist. Chances are, if you have a particular talent, there's a scholarship out there for you.

It's important to keep this definition in mind, since scholarships are different from grants. A grant is like a scholarship, since it's money given to a student to attend college, and, like a scholarship, it doesn't have to be paid back. But grants are usually given based on some kind of demonstrated financial need, while a scholarship is given based on a particular talent. It's easy to confuse the two, especially since some local community groups offer students grants for college, but call them scholarships. This is also true when most students get money for college from the US Government. Students who attend US Military Academies, or veterans who have their education paid by the GI bill, are going to school on a scholarship. Students who receive a Pell Grant or other grant are receiving a grant. We'll discuss grants more in the chapter on Financing a College Education.

Kinds of Scholarships, and Where to Find Them

Private Scholarships

The easiest way to look for scholarships is to break them into two basic types. Private scholarships are the scholarships that get the most attention. These scholarships are usually paid for by a private company (like the Coca-Cola Scholarship and the KFC Colonel's Scholars Program), and each company sets up the rules for who can apply, how to apply, and how recipients are selected. The amount of money available in private scholarships is easily billions of dollars, and that leads students to wonder – if there's so much money out there in private scholarships, why is it so hard to find?

To be honest, private scholarships aren't that hard to find, but they are pretty hard to get. Before the Internet was in wide use (ask your parents about this), finding private scholarships was pretty hard. Unless you happened to know someone who worked for the company offering the scholarship, or unless you camped out in your school counselor's office, there was no way to let everyone know about all of the private scholarships out there.

That all changed with the Internet. Thanks to scholarship sites like Fastweb, Chegg, and Cappex,[1] students can search for scholarships, organize them by subject, add their due dates to an online calendar, and register to get e-mail notices of new scholarships that are added to the website, all for free.

This change has really improved the connection between companies offering private scholarships and the students who need money for college – in fact, the connection is almost too good. With millions of students knowing about the private scholarships that are online, the number of students receiving scholarships is at an all-time high, but so are the number of students applying for the scholarships. This means the chances of any one student receiving the scholarship is usually smaller than ever before. Like those highly selective colleges that only admit a small percentage of students who apply, private scholarships run out of recipients before they run out of great applicants, since there's only so much money to go around.

What can you do to increase the chances you'll earn a private scholarship? Try these steps:

Register on more than one scholarship search site

Most students will only use one of the three websites I've mentioned to search for scholarships. Don't limit yourself; register on all three, and look up other search engines for scholarships, too. There may be some overlap, but this is the best way to find the scholarships listed by only one search engine.

---

[1] See www.fastweb.com, www.chegg.com, and https://www.cappex.com for more information on scholarships. 2/25/2016

Set time aside to do your own searches

Most of these sites will give you a list of scholarships you can apply for, based on the answers you provide to a few questions. That's helpful, but those hard-to-find scholarships can usually only be discovered by setting aside an hour a week just to search through the scholarship lists directly.

Think local

All of the national and international competition for online scholarships is leading more students to go back to the pre-Internet strategy of looking for scholarships in their own communities, where there are fewer students applying for college cash. Community groups like Kiwanis usually offer scholarships, as do local businesses, unions, and foundations that give college scholarships to honor the memory of former community members. Ask around, and look closely.

Be ready to develop a new hobby

You may not have a yo-yo – in fact, you may not even know what one is – but if it meant getting $500 for college, would you figure out where to buy one and practice for a few weeks? That might be all it takes to win a scholarship that isn't well advertised for a hobby that's kind of unusual. Remember, the scholarship doesn't go to the most talented person; it goes to the most talented person who applies for the scholarship.

Another thing to consider when applying for any scholarship are the conditions of being selected. Some private scholarships require the recipients to update the scholarship's sponsor on their college progress, while other company-based scholarships might require you to be included in their advertising, and some community scholarships may have you come back and make a presentation to their organization. Even a yo-yo scholarship may have some strings attached to it; make sure you read the scholarship conditions carefully.

Institutional Scholarships

The second kind of scholarship is institutional scholarships, or scholarships that are given based on the college you attend. When comparing the amounts of money available with each kind of scholarship, there is much more money available through institutional scholarships, with fewer students applying for them, since you can be eligible for the institutional scholarship from the college you attend. The qualifications for institutional scholarships are made by the college, and so are the application process, the selection of the recipients, and any other conditions you have to meet if you receive the scholarship.

One of the most popular types of institutional scholarships is the **merit scholarship**, a scholarship that is awarded based on the student's academic performance in high school. One of the reasons these scholarships are popular is because it's usually easy to determine if you're eligible for them. Most merit scholarships are awarded to any student who earns a specific GPA in high school, or earns a minimum score on the SAT or ACT. These scholarships can run anywhere from a few hundred dollars to covering the entire cost of tuition, books, room and board. Some merit scholarships even include a laptop computer and a research stipend, where the student is paid to go to college.

Finding these merit scholarships has also become easier, thanks to the Internet. The scholarship and financial aid page of any college's website describes their merit aid scholarships in detail, and Cappex has a list of colleges by state that offers merit scholarships. It's always good to double-check the college's website, and make sure they're still offering the merit scholarship described on Chegg. But Chegg is a good place to begin your merit search, since these lists most likely include colleges you've never heard of – and they may have money for you!

Another reason merit scholarships are so popular is because they are usually easy to apply for. In most cases, every student who applies to a college is automatically reviewed for a merit scholarship. The college looks at the student's GPA, test scores, or other information on the college application, compares it to the requirements for the merit scholarship, and then lets the student know if they are eligible for the scholarship. In some cases, this will require the student to complete an extra essay, but it's well worth it, since very few students will bother writing the extra essay – even if it means getting a scholarship.

Scholarship Essays

There are some private and institutional scholarships that require students to complete an extra activity to be considered. In most cases, this extra activity involves writing an essay on a topic related to the scholarship. Many veterans' groups will offer a scholarship to a student who writes the best essay on what America stands for, while a History scholarship offered by a college may require the student to write an essay on the historic event that means the most to them.

It may be hard to believe, but many students who are eligible for scholarships choose not to apply, simply because they don't want to write another essay. Most scholarships essays have a January or February deadline, so students won't apply for them until they're done applying to colleges. Since so many students don't like writing college application essays, the idea of writing even more essays for a scholarship is just too much to think about – so they don't do it.

It's easy to understand why students may get burned out on writing essays. On the other hand, it doesn't do much good to get admitted to college if you don't have the money to pay for college – and that's what the scholarships are for. The best way to avoid essay burnout is to follow the writing tips in the chapter on "Writing an Effective College Application Essay." That will keep you fresh to use these writing strategies when tackling scholarship essays:

Don't be afraid to recycle your college essays

In the chapter on college essays, we said it was more than fine to use the same essay on different college applications, as long as the essay answered both questions effectively – and as long as you change the name of the college. The same is true with scholarship essays. If the scholarship committee wants to know about something that's of value to you, using all or part of your college essay on an experience that had meaning could take care of this scholarship essay. With a few tweaks here and there, you could find new value in that old essay.

Understand what the scholarship essay is looking for

Scholarship prompts often ask the student to do more formal research and writing than college applications – in other words, they may ask for more "head" than "heart." "Pick an historical figure and explain their importance in our world today" is a topic that's commonly used, and a strong answer to this prompt is going to be based on good research of what that person stood for, the contributions they made while they were alive, and how those values are demonstrated today. If it's appropriate, try to personalize the essay at the end by talking about what the historical figure means in your life, but if the prompt wants you to stick to the facts, focus only on those.

Research your scholarships by topic
If you have to write a new essay just for scholarships, make it worth your while. Doing an online search by scholarship topic could help you find a dozen scholarships where the topic is current trends, global warming, patriotism, or our world today. Applying for those scholarships allows you to make the most of your time, and most likely allows you to write the same basic essay that would have to be modified just a little to meet the requirements of one or two of the scholarships.

Consider your audience
The chapter on college essays talked about the importance of writing your essays with a conversational tone. That may not always work with scholarship essays, especially if the essay is expected to have a more academic structure. On the other hand, if this is a local scholarship, and the essay asks you to write about something of meaning to you, there's a good chance you may know members of the community who are on the scholarship committee. If that's the case, write the essay as if you were talking directly to that person. You still want to keep the tone somewhat formal, but if you write you keep that person's interests and knowledge of your life in mind as you write the essay, you'll have an essay that's likely to get more attention.

Emphasize your future plans
Private scholarships – especially local private scholarships – are usually very interested in what you plan to do when you're in college. This is the perfect time to build on the ideas you used in your "Why Us" college application questions. Use specifics to talk about what you plan to study, or why a particular college excites you, or the special program you plan on pursuing, if only you have the money to go to college. Private groups create scholarships so they can help students create futures. If you give them a strong, detailed picture on what your future looks like with their help, your essay is more likely to get noticed.

Proofread, proofread, proofread
It's important to do your best work on any essay, but members of local and private scholarship committees are much more likely to disregard your application if it has a spelling mistake or a typo in it. A

good trick to apply here is to read your essay, correct any errors, and then read the essay again – backwards. Since you're seeing the words in a new order, you're much more likely to spot mistakes this way.

Scholarship Auditions

Students who are hoping to earn a talent-based scholarship are usually used to putting together the presentations they'll be judged by, since many colleges require arts majors to prepare auditions and portfolios for admission to the college. Still, applying for a college can add another layer of stress to the student, since they know this review is for the money they need to go the college they've already been admitted to.

Since scholarship auditions and admission auditions are similar, the best way to prepare for both is to follow these simple guidelines:

Read the requirements carefully

Every audition has its own specific requirements for the kind of music to be performed, the length of the dramatic piece to perform, or the kind of dance moves they'd like to see. Unlike college essays, it's harder to use the same set of pieces for two different auditions or portfolios. Read the directions carefully, and if there's a requirement you don't understand, call the college.

Ask about an advanced tryout

A growing number of colleges are offering artists of all kinds the opportunity to "practice" their audition with feedback from a member of the faculty. Whether in person or through video, these first tries allow students to get some idea on what they should work on before the big tryout – and that first attempt could make a good impression if the real tryout doesn't go as well.

Schedule your auditions wisely

Many colleges will offer more than one set of audition dates, especially for musicians. This leads some students to schedule their audition later, giving them more time to prepare – but if the college makes scholarship decisions on a "first come, first serve" basis, the college could run out of money before the second group of students even has a chance to try out. Ask about this.

Be flexible

If you're about to be the third straight singer at the audition to perform a piece by Adele, you may want to consider doing something else. That only works if you and your accompanist have worked up another song ahead of time. Plan ahead.

Read the conditions of the scholarship closely

You should do this with every scholarship, but it's especially important to do this with a talent scholarship. There may be a certain number of required performances you have to complete that might not fit in with your other plans, or you may have to audition for the scholarship every year. That's good news if you don't get it the first time, but if you do, it's something to keep in mind.

Athletic Scholarships

The world of college sports is so competitive, it's easy for a talented athlete to find themselves in the middle of several interested colleges, well before high school starts. Combine that intense interest with the fact that high school players get injured, and college coaches get fired, and it's hard to determine just what a talented athlete should pay attention to first when thinking about their college scholarship opportunities.

It's best to take this one step at a time. Nearly every college is a member of some kind of league or association that has rules about how, and when, scholarships can be offered. Athletes and their parents should read these recruitment rules carefully, since violating any one of them could make the student ineligible for athletics, and athletic scholarships, at any college. They should also read them every year, since the rules for recruitment, including the kinds of grades and classes high school students must complete, change every year. If you have any interest in college athletics, reading the NCAA requirements starting in seventh grade isn't too soon.[2] If you haven't read them before a college coach contacts you, make sure you read them once they do. You'll also want to work closely with your team coach, who can offer advice on how to work with college coaches.

---

[2] See www.ncaa.org for NCAA requirements.

Recruited athletes will receive invitations to special summer camps and programs, where they will be observed working with other talented athletes of the same age. This is one way athletes audition for a place on the college team, and the best way to prepare for those invitations is to give your best to your sport and to your teammates, no matter where you're playing.

If these invitations lead to a scholarship offer, remember that you must first apply to the college and be admitted before you can accept a scholarship. Also keep in mind that any kind of verbal offer a coach or college makes is never official. The only way you know you've officially been offered a spot on the team, and perhaps a scholarship, is when they give you an offer in writing. Too many coaches make a verbal commitment, only to withdraw that commitment, once they find a player that better meets the needs of the team. If that happens, there's nothing the student can do, unless the offer was in writing.

Finally, remember that nearly every athletic scholarship is good for one year only. That means a scholarship that looked like a sure four-year full ride can be over at any time, due to injury, a change in the coaching staff, or the inability of the student to meet the demands of the coach and the team. And if you aren't recruited for a team, don't worry. Just like many students who earn academic scholarships by finding schools they hadn't heard of, it isn't unusual for non-recruited athletes to walk on, find a spot on the team, and end up with a scholarship the following year. It doesn't happen often at big-name schools, but smaller programs and non-recruited athletes make a perfect fit more often than you think.

More Resources

For a list of additional resources visit:
http://www.thebestschools.org/savvy-students/chapter-resources/

Financing a College Education

The Big Picture

There's certainly no question that college costs a lot of money – much more than when your parents were growing up – and most students aren't going to be able to afford college without a plan, and without some help. While most pre-paid tuition plans are designed for younger students, some can still be of benefit to older students, and a 529 savings plan can help out any student, regardless of age. The process of applying for financial aid is a joint effort among the federal and state governments and the college you'll attend. This partnership often requires a lot of paperwork from students and their families, but it does leave them with some strong payment choices, including some that don't have to include loans. The role of loans is always one to think about carefully, and so is the idea of using some creative approaches to paying for college, including new home mortgages, starting at a community college, and earning college credits while going to high school. All of these options should lead each student to carefully consider if college is the best choice for them, and if so, what kind. At the same time, the advantages of college go beyond the price tag and the financial benefits, a point that is as important now as it ever was.

It used to be that the most challenging part of getting into college was filling out the application on time. All colleges admitted most of their applicants, and with a strong summer job and a little of Mom and Dad's savings, college could be paid for, books and all.

Things have certainly changed. A number of colleges now admit less than 20 percent of the students who apply, and more students who are admitted to any college are looking for some kind of financial help as ever before.

Looking at the many ways to pay for college may be daunting at first, but with a little patience and a few strong websites, you'll soon discover you don't need a college degree in Business to figure out how to pay for your college degree in anything.

Savings Plans

If you're a student reading this, you might be thinking "OK, something I can skip. Mom and Dad didn't buy one of those pre-paid plans when I was young, so this isn't for me."

A number of states do offer savings plans that get you the biggest return if they're purchased early, but there are also some that can realize big savings now. Just in case you have a much younger brother or sister, you can find a list of states that offer a pre-paid tuition program.[1] Since these are all state-based plans, they each have their own rules and limitations, so you'll want to read the rules carefully for the one in your state – but in general, here's how they work:

- Someone (usually a parent) buys a pre-paid contract for tuition from the state they live in.
- When it's time for someone else (you) to go to college, the pre-paid contract is used to pay for tuition. These contracts usually apply only for public colleges and universities in your state, and they usually don't cover room board, books, or personal expenses.
- If the student chooses to attend a private college in the state, or go to college outside the state, the investor usually gets their investment back, plus some interest. The amount is often based either on the average tuition rate at state colleges at the time, or the average rate of return of the investment since it was purchased.

The rate of return also varies by state, and by program, so there are a few that can be purchased when the student is older that might still be a good investment. This is something to check with each individual plan.

No matter how old the student is, and even if the parents have bought a pre-paid contract, many states also offer a 529 savings plan.[2] These plans work a little differently than pre-paid tuition:

- Someone (usually a parent) opens a 529 savings account in the name of the student.

---

[1] See www.finaid.org/savings/state529plans.phtml for a list of pre-paid tuition programs. 2/25/2016

[2] See www.finaid.org/savings/state529plans.phtml for a list of savings plans. 2/25/2016

- At any time, the parent makes deposits to the savings account (some programs have annual and lifetime maximums), where the money earns interest.
- In many cases, the deposits can be used as tax deductions or tax credits on the parent's state income tax (but not on their federal tax).
- The interest earned on the deposits is tax free, provided all deposits are used for educationally-related expenses.
- Some states will allow the name of the beneficiary to change, so if one child doesn't go to college, the money can be used by another child, or even by the parent.

Some families choose to start both a pre-paid tuition plan and a 529 plan, so they can begin to save for both tuition (pre-paid tuition) and other college expenses (529 plan). Either way, the question comes up – are these plans better investments than if the parents simply took the money and invested it in the stock market, or with a financial planner?

A quick look at the summaries of the effect of these plans suggests the answer is – it depends. Many states have different kinds of investment plans with different levels of possible return and possible risk, leaving it up to the investor to decide what plan best suits their comfort level. In addition, some families feel they need the structure of an official college plan to make sure they set something aside for college. Many of these families don't have other investments, or they feel that, if they did, it would be too tempting to use a general investment fund for something else, like a trip to Disney World.

On the other hand, general investments aren't a sure thing either, and any investment with a financial planner involves fees to pay them. Then again, some students feel limited by their college choice if their parents invest in a pre-paid tuition program. Sure, they will still get their money back, plus a little more (usually), but that kind of seems to defeat the purpose of having the tuition paid up front.

Families considering these plans should look carefully at the specific rate of return and limitations of the benefits – but either way, they need to start saving for college. When the cost of college was soaring about twenty years ago, there was a feeling the government would intervene in some way, and offer free college for everyone. That plan is still being talked about, but it doesn't seem to be coming any time soon – and families qualifying for current federal aid generally need something more to pay the full college bill. So look at your options, and start saving – if you end up going to college for free, you could always use the money for something else, like a trip to Disney World.

Applying for Assistance in Paying for College

Whether you've put money away for college or not, it's likely you're going to apply for help to pay for college. The process is easy to describe, and requires help from your parents. Ready?

Complete the FAFSA
The Free Application for Federal Student Aid (FAFSA) is the first step in applying for financial assistance with college. Created and maintained by the federal government, the answers you give on FAFSA are first sent to the US Government, where they determine if you qualify for any of the federal assistance programs. These programs fall into three categories: **Grants**, or need-based money you receive that you don't have to pay back, as long as you keep your grades up; **Work study**, where you work about 10 hours a week at your college, and most (or all) of your paycheck goes back to the college to pay for tuition; and **Loans**, or money you use to pay for college that you must pay back.

Generally speaking, until the student turns 24, they have to complete the FAFSA using both their income information, and their parent's income information. It doesn't matter to the government if you're not living with your parents, or if they have refused to pay for college, even if they have the money. In most cases, their incomes will be taken into consideration when you apply for aid.[3]

Once the federal government receives your FAFSA, they generate a number called the Expected Family Contribution, or EFC. The EFC is then shared with your state, and with the colleges you've applied to. Some states, and each college, have their own financial aid resources they can use to help students pay for college, so once they get your EFC, they try to figure out how much help they can give you.

---

[3]To see the exceptions, which are important, take a look at the Federal Student Aid website at https://studentaid.ed.gov/sa/, which has everything you need to know about federal financial aid.

An example should help here. Let's say your family completes the FAFSA, and the federal government says your family can spend $10,000 a year on college. That's your Expected Family Contribution, or EFC.

You want to go to a college where the cost of attendance (that's tuition, room and board, books, and personal fees) is $15,000. Since you can only pay $10,000, you need $5000 more to go to college.

After you complete the FAFSA, the federal government decides you qualify for $1000 in grant, $1600 in work study, and $1000 in loan. That's $3500 in aid of the $5000 you need, meaning you need another $1400.

At this point, all that information is shared with the college. They may want more information about your finances, so they might ask you to complete another financial aid form – usually the CSS Profile[4] or a form they've created. The college will then look at the money they have to offer students, and try to find the $1400 you need. That could be more grant, more work study, more loan, or a merit-based scholarship (we talk about those in another chapter).

Complications in Paying for College

If this all sounds pretty easy, it's supposed to be – but it can get complicated in a hurry, especially if one of the following happens:

You don't fill out the FAFSA

Many parents refuse to fill out the FAFSA, either because they think it's too confusing, or they are sure they won't qualify for federal financial aid. It's certainly true that not many families qualify for help from the US Government – but if you don't try, very few colleges will give you any money, until they know Uncle Sam isn't going to pay for college. In terms of the FAFSA being pretty complicated, it is, at least for right now. But if you have your income tax information from last year, the form takes about an hour to complete – and a number of colleges and tax preparers participate in a program called College Goal, where they will help you fill out the FAFSA for free.

---

[4] See https://student.collegeboard.org/css-financial-aid-profile.

You don't complete the other financial aid forms your college needs

Some parents are OK with sharing their financial information with the US Government, but won't fill out the more detailed CSS Profile to give to the colleges. Many schools need that information to see if the student qualifies for money that has special restrictions, so without the extra information, you won't get the extra cash.

You can't really pay what the EFC says you can pay

One of the biggest complaints of the current FAFSA is that most families can't pay the Expected Family Contribution – the amount is simply too high. The college's financial aid office is usually willing to hear about the circumstances that make it impossible for families to pay the EFC, but it is a problem that is happening more and more.

You don't get all the aid you need

In our example, the student needed $1400 in aid from the college in order to go to school. But what if the college only gave the student $500 – or nothing at all? The student would have to make up the difference, or the "gap", between what they need, and the aid they've received. This is happening more and more, and the gap usually isn't in the hundreds of dollars – it's in the thousands.

You don't want to take out any loans for college

With all of the stories going around about students who graduated with a Bachelor's degree and $100,000 in debt, it's easy to understand why students don't want to start their lives with debt from college. Given the high cost of everything, paying off a loan in an uncertain job market is something you just don't want to think about.

So what do you do if you don't want any loans? Well, don't accept them. When you get a financial aid offer from the government or from a college, it's just that – an offer. You can turn down the loan and keep the other two parts; you can turn down the loan and the work study, and just take the grant; if you'd like, you can turn down the whole thing. It's important to remember that, if you turn down part of an offer, you aren't going to get a different offer where they increase the grant. You're just saying that you don't want that part, and you're going to figure out some other way to cover that expense.

Other Factors to Consider
It's always wise to think twice before taking out a loan for anything. But as you consider the role of loans in paying for college, consider these factors:

Your income once you finish college
Dan (not his real name) graduated with a degree in Chemical Engineering and $29,000 in debt (that's about the average for a four-year degree). That's a lot of money – but since the average starting salary of chemical engineers is $66,400, there's a good chance Dan can afford the monthly payment of a loan that he's going to repay over 30 years. In fact, unless Dan has a ridiculous life style, he should be able to pay that loan off in 5 years – and remember, the only way he could earn such a great starting salary is by taking the loans out in the first place.

The job you have once you finish
Cindy (not her real name) graduated with $15,000 in debt, but she's a teacher, and her starting salary is $34,000 (about the national average). Cindy can't afford to pay her debt off in five years, but she can afford the monthly payment for five years – and since she's a teacher, that means the rest of her federal student loan will be forgiven, as long as she's still teaching in the school where she's working now.

Other options
Bill (you get the idea) didn't want to take out a $6,000 loan for his first year in college, but because he kept his grades up and was active in his residence hall, he was selected to be a residence hall advisor the following year. At his college, that job comes with free room and board, which more than replaced the need for Bill to take out any more loans for college.

It's easy to look at situations like Bill's and Cindy's and think, well, those were special situations. But when it comes to paying for college, everyone has special circumstances. It's too easy to think that you're destined to become one of those unemployed students with insane college debt who ends up living on your parent's couch. If you look closely at your college options, and look closely at the tips on getting scholarships in the next chapter, you're likely to find that you may have a special situation of your own – and that might include where it's OK to take out a college loan.

As you consider your borrowing options, you want to make especially sure to keep a close eye on using private loans or PLUS loans as part of your payment strategies. Unlike federal loans that often don't have to be paid back until you're done with college, most private loans require you start making payments right away, just like a car loan or a house loan. While PLUS loans have favorable repayment plans, they also have a very high ceiling – your parents can borrow up to the full cost of college if they qualify. That may sound good in the short term, but any family should think twice about borrowing the full cost of college. There are likely better ways to achieve that goal.

Other Approaches to Affording College

The high cost of college, and the recent Great Recession, led many families to look at creative ways to pay for college. These may not work for you, but they're certainly worth considering:

Home equity or remortgaging
Parents who are used to making monthly house payments sometimes decide to use the equity they have in their house to pay for college, or to get a new mortgage on their home. Since the payment is already built into their monthly budget, they see this as a way to afford college without having to change their lifestyle. This way of paying for college could have an effect on when your parents will retire, so it's important for them to consider their entire financial picture before using this approach.

Starting at a community college and transferring
This strategy was extremely popular in the economic downturn of 2008, and with good reason. Since community college tuition is usually much lower than that of most four-year colleges, students begin their college careers locally and live at home, saving the money of room and board as well. With a year or two of transferrable credits, the student completes their four-year degree at a four year institution – and if they did well at community college, they may qualify for a Phi Theta Kappa scholarship as a distinguished community college student.

This approach has worked for thousands of students, but it's important to do your homework. Not every community college class will transfer to a four-year college, and some will only transfer as elective credits, something you don't need much of when earning a Bachelor's degree. The best way to make sure the classes you take locally will help you at the four year college is to talk with the transfer advisor at the four-year school. The advice you get from the school accepting the credits is all that matters.

Earning college credit in high school

Many colleges will give credit to students who have earned high scores on Advanced Placement (AP), International Baccalaureate (IB), and College-Level Examination Program (CLEP) exams. Students generally prepare for these tests while taking accelerated courses in high school, and while the exams aren't free, a good score can more than pay for itself with the college credit the student will earn. Not every college accepts these tests, so again, you'll want to talk with the transfer coordinator at the four-year college you plan on attending.

Other high-school based programs that offer college credit include **dual enrollment** or **early college** programs. Dual enrollment occurs when a student takes some high school classes and some college classes while still in high school – but in this case, the college classes are paid for by the local school district or the state. Most early college programs operate the same way, but the students takes a specific set of college classes (some of them offered at the high school) in order to earn an Associate's Degree either at the same time they graduate from high school, or one year later. Credits from these programs don't always transfer to four-year colleges, so it's best to ask in advance.

Attend a free college

Plans may be underway to offer free college to everyone, but there are some colleges that are free to all students right now, while others are free to many.[5] Note that many require students to complete required work study as a condition of enrollment. This list doesn't include the US military academies, which are also free, but do require all graduates to complete a number of years in military service after graduation.

---

[5]A strong list of these colleges can be found at http://www.thebestschools.org/magazine/tuition-free-colleges/

Is College Worth It?

It costs more to go to college now than ever before, so much so that many are wondering if the value of a college education is as strong as it once was. Where a Bachelor's Degree of any kind was once a guarantee to a better paying job, that just isn't the case anymore. In fact, some argue, there are higher paying jobs in the technical trades where you can earn more than someone working as a barista with a Bachelor's Degree.

Deciding if college is worth it is really an individual decision, for two reasons. First, the Bureau of Labor Statistics continues to tell us what has long been true. On average, the more education you have, the more money you will make – and, just as important, the more education you have, the less likely you are to be out of a job at any time in your life. These are averages, of course, and there are exceptions, but even after nearly a decade of high college costs, the investment in a college degree of any kind is still worth it economically.

The second reason college is worth it has to do with a different kind of value. With more kinds of classes to offer and experiences like study abroad available to nearly every student, college plays an important role in making sure students understand just how big, and different, the world is around them. That alone may not be worth taking on thousands of dollars of debt, but combined with the career opportunities still only available through college, the ability to understand more about the world, and more about the people we live with in the world, are valuable skills to have in the work we do, the families we raise, and the neighbors we live with. There's more to everyone's life than the job they have and the taxes they pay. One or more years of college is an important reminder of that, giving students the skills not only to contribute to our world, but to improve it.

More Resources

For a list of additional resources visit:
http://www.thebestschools.org/savvy-students/chapter-resources/

Benefits and Pitfalls of Student Loans

The Big Picture

Students thinking about taking out loans to pay for college usually fall into one of two categories. Either they are more than willing to take out any amount they need, or they are too terrified of not being able to pay back the loan to even think about taking one out. The best way to consider if a student loan is right for you is to get an understanding of the purpose of loans in general, and understand how they work. From there, students should consider the reasons why a student loan would create a stronger college choice for them – or, in some cases, create a college choice. It's then important to understand how the unexpected can make it more challenging to pay back student loans, which can affect a student's credit history, and their ability to provide for themselves and their family as an adult. In the end, four key questions should drive the decision to borrow for college, and how much to borrow for college, remembering that money is a factor in making a good college choice, but not the only factor.

It's almost impossible to think about going to college without thinking about students loans. In a way, that's a very good thing, since a loan of any kind has an impact on our lives for many, many years, and it's important not to do anything that has a long-lasting effect on our lives without thinking about it for a while.

At the same time, it would be pretty easy to listen to older friends in college and some family members and think that you should never take out student loans, no matter what. People often give that advice because they want to make sure you don't end up owing more in student loans than you can afford to pay back, especially if you don't finish college with a certificate or a degree that helps you get a good-paying job. But automatically saying "no" to a student loan is almost as bad as automatically saying "yes" to a student loan. Without considering the advantages that come with a student loan, as well as the commitment you're making when taking one out, you're really just guessing about your future – and that's just as bad as picking a college without visiting the campus.

Like any other part of the college selection process, deciding whether or not to take a student loan requires information and research, so let's take a look at the world of student loans, and see what might make you decide it's worth doing to meet your life goals, or something you're better off living without.

What is a Loan?

Most high school students have only heard about the loans their parents have taken out, to buy things like cars or houses, or to start a business. These are great examples of why people borrow money – to get something right away that they are willing to pay extra for once they get it. Most loans are given for big purchases – like houses – where it would take a very long time to save all the money needed to pay for something in cash. Instead of doing that, the purchaser decides to borrow some of the money they need to buy the house (or car), and pays the loan back in small amounts over a large period of time. Some of each payment goes towards paying off the loan, and some of each payment is interest, or extra money the lender gets for loaning you the money to begin with.

The interest part of a loan can easily be seen as a reason not to borrow money, since paying interest increases the cost of whatever you're buying. Let's say you want to borrow $25,000 to buy a new car at an interest rate of just over 3%. You would get the car right away, and each month for the next 5 years, you would pay $450 a month to pay off that loan. At the end of that time, the car is yours to keep, sell, or do whatever you'd like with, and you would have paid $27.026 to pay the loan back – so the car would cost you an extra $2,026.

Since it doesn't make sense to pay more for something if you can get it for a lower price, some people wonder why someone would take out a loan to pay for anything. In this case, it's likely the person taking out the car loan doesn't have $25,000 in cash, and they either need – or want – the car right away. If they have a job where they make enough money that the lender believes they can afford the monthly payment, it's much easier for some people to repay $450 a month at a time to a lender than it is for them to put $450 in a savings account each month for 56 months. With that much money, they might decide to spend it on other things, like a vacation, and never have enough money to buy a car in cash. This is especially true if someone is buying a house. With the average price of a house at about $185,000, it would take someone over 34 years to save $450 a month to buy that house in cash.

Benefits of Student Loans

The basic ideas of a loan make a great deal of sense when you think you need money for college. There aren't many brand new high school graduates who have $24,000 in cash to pay for the average year of college by themselves,[1] and many families find it hard to save for college while paying for food, cars, housing, and medical care, especially when the US economy was doing so badly for many years. This is one of the reasons why 7 out of 10 students recently graduating from college had $28,000 in debt that came from taking out student loans.[2]

What would lead someone to decide to take out that much money for college? It can be any one of these reasons:

It prepared them for a better-paying job

It surprises many students, but one of the best ways to make more money is to borrow money for college. The Bureau of Labor Statistics[3] shows that the average four-year college graduate makes nearly twice the monthly salary of someone who only has a high school diploma. Even when compared to students who take some college classes but don't earn a degree, four-year college graduates make nearly twice as much in salary – and their unemployment rate is a little more than half, meaning they are much more likely to be employed.

It allowed them to have a longer college experience

Some families are able to save enough for a student to attend one or two years of school, but if their child is looking for a four-year college

---

[1] That includes tuition, room and board, and books and fees, according to http://www.collegedata.com/cs/content/content_payarticle_tmpl.jhtml?articleId=10064
[2] http://www.usnews.com/news/articles/2014/11/13/average-student-loan-debt-hits-30-000
[3] http://www.bls.gov

experience, a student loan can make all the difference. Those two extra years of school can also make a difference once the student graduates, since four-year degree holders make about 40 percent more than graduates with a two-year degree.

It let them live away from home

Most people are surprised to discover that the average cost of college tuition is about $9500. That's still a lot of money, but it's much less than the average $24,000 that includes room and board. This means that a student living at home during their four years of college can save a lot of money, even when adding in books and the cost of keeping up a car to drive back and forth to school.

Living at home during college has many advantages, but for some students, living on their own is part of the college experience that's very important to them. In addition to being able to sleep in (when they don't have class) and stay up late, living away from home gives students the opportunity to interact with roommates from different towns, states, or countries. It also gives the student the chance to learn how to manage time between school, social activities, and life activities like doing laundry, shopping for food, and managing their own budget. For many students – and for some parents – living away from home while going to college is just as meaningful, and as much of an education, as the classes the students takes. For families who feel that way, taking out student loans to pay for this important experience is an easy decision to make.

It gave them a different college experience

Students who are admitted to more than one college are in the challenging position of comparing what each college has to offer, and deciding which one is a best "fit", or the one that best meets all of their needs and interests. In deciding among different colleges, cost isn't the only factor, but it certainly is one factor many students consider. The average cost of attending college may be $24,000, but that means there are many colleges that cost much more than that. If a student is admitted to two colleges, and one costs much more than the other, is it really worth the difference – even if that means taking out loans to attend the more expensive school?

For some students, the answer is yes. The more expensive school may have a better reputation for the program the student wants to study, and that could lead to better job prospects after graduation, or a richer learning experience during college. When comparing factors like the number of internships each college offers, or where those internships are offered, students often feel the quality of the more expensive college is worth taking out loans to afford.

Many students looking at a difference in price between two schools are looking at a public college that's less expensive, and a private college that has a smaller class size, but a higher price tag. In this case, some students feel the private college is a must, since they are more successful students when they are in classes with fewer students. In this case, student loans may make an important difference in their college choice. At the same time, these students will also want to look into the residential or honors college options at their public universities, since these programs often have smaller class sizes available to students who qualify for these advanced programs. These specialized opportunities may also have special scholarships available for qualified students, giving the student additional financial support for college that doesn't have to be paid back.

Finally, other students may choose the smaller learning environment that's more expensive just because the school feels more comfortable to them. Feeling at home is certainly an important part of the college experience, but it isn't the only part of the decision, since too much comfort might not inspire the student to challenge themselves to go out and meet new people, or make the most of the learning experiences at college. Students should also remember that many colleges allow students to live off campus after their first or second year at college. This gives the student the chance to spend a little more on housing, while still enjoying the savings of a low tuition college. These decisions are part of the student's personal preferences, but it's important to remember that if those preferences are being funded with student loans, there are long-term consequences to the choices the student makes.

It let them go to college

There are a growing number of students who simply don't have the money and other resources they need to go to college without borrowing money to do so. For many of these students, borrowing this much money before they begin their careers can be a little scary, and that makes sense. But to them, not going to college at all seems even scarier, since college can lead to the personal and professional growth they need to understand more about the world, contribute more to the world, and make a better life for themselves and their family. This doesn't mean they should borrow money they don't need, and it doesn't mean they should automatically go to the most expensive college that admits them, but if a student loan is the difference between a well-thought out college choice and no college at all, the choice can be pretty easy to make for many students.

Pitfalls of Student Loans

Borrowing money at any stage of your life should be a reason to think very carefully about why you're borrowing the money, and if you really need it. This is especially true if you don't really know how you're going to pay the money back. Failing to pay back a student loan (also known as defaulting) can lead to having paychecks taken away from you, a bad credit rating that will keep you from getting credit cards or other loans, and more.

Students can't always predict the future – no one can – but it is important to think about the following factors before you borrow, since your answers to many of these issues can help determine if you're going to pay back your loan:

You change your major, which leads to a different career choice

You decided to take a student loan to pay for a more expensive college experience. Since you planned on becoming an Engineer, you were pretty sure your starting salary (usually around $70,000) would give you more than enough money to pay off your student loans – in fact, you'd likely have enough money to pay it off early.

The plan was going pretty well, until you got a D in your first semester of Physics in college, and fell in love with the idea of being a teacher instead, where the starting salary is much lower. You might qualify for some loan forgiveness if you teach in high need schools for several years, but paying your bills and your loans is going to be harder on this lower salary.

Part of the college experience involves trying out new classes, and thinking about new careers. But if your college financial plan is built around a high-paying career, either the plan will limit the new classes you can consider, or the new classes could make your payment plan more difficult. Make an honest assessment of your interest in your major before you bet too much of your future on it.

You try out your career, but just don't like it

The same problem can come up once you're done with college, and you go into the field you studied in college – what happens when working as an accountant, day after day, doesn't turn out to be as interesting as it seemed when you were doing something new as an intern every week? It can be hard to look four or five years ahead and decide if you're going to like your job, but job shadowing and research can give you some clues, and if you aren't sure, don't bank your college payment plan on a big paycheck.

Your family's financial situation changed

This happened to thousands of college students during the Great Recession. Your family had saved enough for you to attend a public university, and you decided to take out student loans to attend a private college instead. Suddenly, one parent loses a job, or their investments lose a lot of value, and now you'll need to take out even more loans just to complete college at a public university – and that's if your credits will transfer. There's a difference between using student loans in an emergency, and using them to buy something you can't otherwise afford. Make sure you understand which way you're using them.

You transfer colleges

More than a few students find their first-choice college isn't everything they thought it was going to be, and it makes sense to transfer to another college if that's the case, especially if you're transferring to a less expensive college. But many transfer students find that not all of their credits will transfer from one college to another, which increases the number of semesters you'll be in college – and that increases the size of your student loans. If there isn't room in your long-term plan for more loan, your college plans are now in peril.

The terms of the loan change in ways you hadn't expected

You were so excited to finally find a bank that would be willing to give you a loan for college, so you signed the papers and headed off to campus. That month, you were surprised to receive your first payment notice for the loan. It turns out this loan didn't have a deferral option, where you could wait to start paying on the loan until you finished college. It also turns out the interest rate is much higher, since it wasn't a loan that was subsidized by the US government. The loan you wanted may have had those options, but the loan you received has none of those. You now have to go back to work to pay for a loan you took out for college – but since you didn't understand the terms of the loan, you have to quit college to pay back your college loan.

You don't finish college

Too many students who borrow money for college think they don't have to pay the money back if they don't earn a degree or certificate. They think that they can simply stop going to school if it gets too hard, and someone else will take care of the loan.

This is a hard lesson for many students to learn, but any money you borrow for school has to be paid back, whether you finish college or not. It doesn't really matter what the reason is; if the work is too hard, if you get sick, if your parents need you back home, you've still borrowed money for college, and that money has to be paid back.

Four Questions when Borrowing for College

Some students get so excited about having the chance to make their college dreams come true, they don't pay any attention to the amount of debt they go into to make it happen. Other students read about all of the unknowns of borrowing to pay for college, and decide they shouldn't borrow a single cent for school, even if it means not going.

All students, and parents, who are considering student loans for college should let these four questions guide their decision to take out student loans for college:

Have I used up every other reasonable source to pay for college?

Everyone has a different mix of income, savings, investments, and assets, so there isn't one single way to address this question. What's important is that each family looks at the resources they have to pay for college, and the cost of the college options they have, and make as good a match as possible. This may include borrowing, and it may not, but it needs to include a discussion of factors other than affordability. If a less expensive college is a bad fit, a loan may be the right thing to do.

Are we borrowing the absolute maximum we can, or are leaving some room for an emergency?

Any family that needs to take out a loan should always leave room for the unexpected, and that's definitely the case with student loans for college. Having no resources to tend to a sudden illness or personal issue adds significant stress to the student, and that increases the chances they will do poorly in college, or drop out completely. Be sure to leave some financial wiggle room.

Would we be better off taking out loans in the parent's name?

Most student loans that have deferred payment plans and subsidized interest rates have to be taken out in the student's name, but there may be some situations where parents are better off taking out loans rather than disturbing long-standing investments. Make sure you understand all of your options before committing to a loan.

How will the student pay these loans back?

Many of the jobs of the future haven't been invented yet, making it even harder for students to create a plan for paying back student loans that is guaranteed to work. On the other hand, maxing out your student loans with the idea that you'll pay them back "someday" isn't the best approach, either. Students should research the starting salaries of at least a few careers, and run some numbers through a student loan calculator[4] to get some kind of understanding of the future financial commitment they're making. This exercise can also be an eye opener to students who have never thought about what it costs to pay rent, insurance, utilities and food. Seeing student loan repayment as part of a bigger picture can only help them make a stronger, more-informed college choice.

More Resources

For a list of additional resources visit:
http://www.thebestschools.org/savvy-students/chapter-resources/

---

[4]see http://www.finaid.org/calculators/loanpayments.phtml for an example

Career Prospects of Different Majors

The Big Picture

It's easy to fall in love with a job and find out the many degree options that could prepare you for that job – but what do you do if you fall in love with a major in college, but don't know where that will lead in the world of work? A carefully outlined three-step process will help you understand how to convert your college studies into job prospects, and that process starts by becoming familiar with the many programs available through your college's career placement program, including their major-career match website. Combined with a review of websites run by professional organizations related to your major, and a quick read of mainstream media articles on your major, it's easy to make some connections between your college studies and your plan of work, all while remembering the seven key career areas that tend to be available at one level or another, regardless of what you study – teaching, journalism, business, entrepreneurship, government, technology, or avocation/hobby, where you follow your love of your major on your own time, while finding a job in another field that meets your financial needs.

In the chapter "Selecting a College Major," we talked about ways to discover different kinds of college majors, and ways to track careers back to certain majors. In this chapter, we're going to turn things around a little, and look at how to discover the careers that are tied to specific majors. We won't be able to talk about every major, but we'll use a system and point you to the right resources that will allow you to investigate the career options of any major, and discuss some careers that are available to you with any major, as long as you have a degree.

Exploring Careers Online

Thanks to the Internet, it's easier than ever before to get information on career options, based on your college major. A number of the easiest sites to use are tied to the career services pages of colleges and universities. This is one of the best programs available at most colleges, but most students don't even think of using it until they are close to graduating, or out in the world of work. Career services (also known in some colleges as placement services) offers information about how to select a major, how to investigate careers, how to search for jobs, how to build a resume, how to prepare for an interview, and more. All of these services are usually free to students, and many are free to graduates for their first year out in the workforce. Many career service programs also host companies and employers on campus, giving students the opportunity to interview for jobs with national and international firms without ever having to leave campus.

The key is to visit career services in your first few weeks on campus, since the best way to make the most out of the services they offer is to know what's offered, and the best times in your college career to use each service.

A look at some of the career placement websites shows some different approaches to connecting majors with possible careers.[1] The career services website of the University of Washington, offers a list of possible areas of employment, the major employers within each area, and strategies for pursuing those specific jobs.[2] General employability strategies for the major are also listed, offering insights to students on what they should be focusing on in college in addition to the knowledge they're obtaining in the classroom. For example, when discussing careers in accounting, UW suggests students consider joining the accounting and finance fraternity Beta Alpha Psi, and urges students to develop personal skills that are valued in accounting careers, including teamwork, communication, and problem-solving skills.[3]

A quick comparison of the What Can I Do with This Major website to the University of Washington site shows much of the same

---

[1] The career service websites of a number of colleges point students to the easy-to-remember website, http://whatcanidowiththismajor.com/major/.

[2] See http://careers.uw.edu/Students/What-Can-I-Do-With-a-Major-In

[3] http://careers.uw.edu/sites/default/files/all/editors/docs/students/whatcanidowith_accounting.pdf

information, but What Can I do With This Major also offers links to related websites, including professional associations, information on job availability from the Occupation Outlook Handbook,[4] and job postings. If you're wondering about the Occupation Outlook Handbook, it offers solid information about job statistics and availability, but it doesn't offer much in the way of connecting college majors to careers. We'll talk more about OOH in another chapter, where the structure of this information-rich site really shines.

Still other career service websites offer students more detailed information on each career related to the major, introducing the student to the kind of work done, a summary of the job requirements, points of interest related to the work (including information on starting salaries), and the top employers nationally in each of the fields.[5]

A number of professional associations offer advice on the careers available in their field based on the major a student has. The American Psychological Association devotes a big piece of its website to careers for students with degrees in psychology,[6] talking about the jobs available at each degree level, and explaining each different field available to psychologists. Sites like Engineer Girl go beyond general information and focus on the opportunities available to women with degrees in Engineering, including advice on how to prepare for the major.[7] In exploring these options, make sure you're looking for information that tells you what jobs you can get with the degree, not what degree you need for a specific job. These are two different questions, and we'll talk about the second one in just a minute.

Finally, the degree-major connection is being picked up more and more by the media, where magazines and online media will offer short, focused stories on what students can do with a specific degree. Most of these stories focus on how much money each job will pay, and offers a brief overview of the nature of the work, along with an estimate of the need for workers in each field.[8] These articles can be a great introduction into a field, but serious students will want to add to this

---

[4]http://www.bls.gov/ooh/
[5]This is the approach taken at myplan.com (http://www.myplan.com/majors/what-to-do-with-a-major.php), which serves as both a connection between majors and careers and a career awareness site.
[6]http://www.apa.org/action/careers/facts.aspx
[7]http://www.engineergirl.org/
[8]As an example, see http://www.therichest.com/business/salary/the-best-jobs-to-get-with-a-business-degree/?view=all)

information by visiting a career services website that offers more detailed information about the major.

Given all of these resources, what's the best way to get clear, up-to-date information on the job prospects for a degree you're interested in? Follow these steps:

- Look up the degree using any of the career service websites. Most will lead you to What Can I do With This Major, so you might just want to start there.
- Look up the websites of any professional organizations associated with your major. These websites may talk more about the different degrees that lead to the same job, but at this point in your search, that's OK. You may be better off with a different major than the one you had in mind, if you want to secure a certain job.
- At this point, really open things up, and do a website search on "Careers for a _____ Degree." You may end up with more career service sites, but you may stumble across a feature article or another professional website that offers a different take on your career. If this search is too large, try "Careers for a _____ Degree in (name of your state)." This can give you some detailed information on the job prospects that are unique to your area.

As you complete your research, keep in mind that many websites will only provide partial lists of job possibilities. This is especially true with feature stories or magazine articles, where they sell the "exciting" jobs to the reader, or the jobs that pay the highest salaries. The financial side of a job is certainly an important one to consider, but it isn't the only factor to keep in mind when selecting a major and a career. There are many rich people who are unhappy with their career choices, while others who make far less in their paychecks go to work each day with a sense of excitement and purpose. Focus on the websites that include detailed discussions on the nature of the work; those will lead you to making the best choices.

Choices No Matter What Your Major

Every major has career choices that are unique to the skills, applications, and solutions unique to that major. At the same time, there are some jobs that are available to almost every degree. While these jobs may vary in availability and pay, each of them is worth considering as you investigate any major, to see if there's a major-career fit for you.

Teaching

It's safe to say that any major where you earn a degree needs teachers, since the only way you earned that degree was to take classes from people who taught you in that field. The nature of education is always changing, but there is always going to be a need for those who guide, encourage, and instruct students, whether it's in a traditional classroom, online, or through guided independent study.

Elementary and Secondary School

The need for teachers in grades K-12 isn't as big right now, but it's heading for an upswing around 2024, as the birth rate continues to rise. Elementary teachers usually have to major in education, but many middle school and high school teachers complete their teaching qualifications by earning a degree in their area of expertise and completing one additional year of teacher training. This means that, as long as you have a degree in something that's taught in grades 6-12, there's a good chance you can become a teacher.

Community College

Community college attendance enjoyed a big increase during the economic downturn, as thousands of people who were suddenly laid off needed new technical or career training, and fast. That trend has died down as people are now back at work, but another trend is growing – students who attend one or two years of community college to save on college, then transfer to a four-year college to finish their degree.

Whether they go for training or transfer, community college students need instructors, and most community colleges will hire instructors who have a Master's degree or more in their field – and if you're in a technical field, you may be able to teach with just a Bachelor's degree. Many community colleges are starting to hire only part-time instructors, so making a career out of teaching at this level may require taking two or more part-time jobs, but if teaching at the college level is of interest, this is worth looking into – and since community colleges offer classes in more fields, there's a better chance you hold a degree in a field where they need teachers.

Four-year colleges

Almost all instructors at four-year colleges and universities hold what's called a terminal degree, or the highest degree that's available in their field. For most majors, that's a doctorate of some kind, but some majors stop at the Master's level.

Positions at four-year colleges and universities differ from community college positions. Faculty at four-year colleges usually teach less than instructors at community colleges, spending the rest of their time focusing on writing and research. If you'd rather spend your time working with students than doing experiments, community college teaching might be a better opportunity for you.

Like community college positions, full-time teaching jobs at a four-year college are becoming harder to find, so qualified candidates will have to have plenty of part-time (or adjunct) teaching experience and research background in order to secure a job.

Community education and private instruction

While many teachers look for full-time positions, other instructors look to teaching as a way to share something they love with just a few students at a time on a part-time basis. For these teachers, working through community education programs to teach workshops or short-term classes is one way to share their knowledge, while others will offer private lessons or tutoring to small groups of students or individuals. Teachers choosing this option will need to be real self-starters who are willing to reach out to existing community programs and propose new courses, do their own advertising and promotion, and keep track of their own expenses and income. This area of teaching isn't limited to an area where you hold a degree, as many teaching positions are available for teachers who have an expertise in hobbies like skydiving, woodcarving, and knitting.

Journalism

The traditional path to a career as a journalist has changed almost as quickly as the number of ways we get news. While the one sure way to having your name appear on an article read by thousands every day used to be a degree in Journalism, a different path of academic preparation is starting to emerge.

To be sure, a journalism degree is still a prime qualification for those seeking full-time employment at a newspaper, as well as most magazines. It's uncertain just how long the print editions of these media are going to last, but if they eventually fade away, their online versions are still going to be largely written by people who have studied writing, communication, and the ethics of being the public's eyes and ears.

At the same time, a growing amount of internet space, including online newspapers, is being turned over to writers who have an expertise in a field, and write about it. These authors (it's best not to call them reporters for now) generally have a degree in the field they're writing about (medicine, education, politics, the arts), and have taken enough writing courses to know how to do research, check sources, and offer insights that are as balanced as their publisher wants them to be.

This second approach to writing about the news is especially popular in the world of technology, where changes occur so rapidly, and at such depths, it's nearly impossible to understand just what's going on without a degree in the field. This is also the case with medicine, and with other areas that may not be in the news very often, but rely on a deep amount of expertise when they do.

Either path can lead to some kind of employment, and no matter which one you take, the time to start writing is now. From the school newspaper to the blogosphere, there is always room for a thoughtful voice who does their research and offers both sides of the story. There's no need to wait for college to begin developing your voice, and you don't even have to have a major before you start sharing your ideas with the world. All you need is an interest in why things are the way they are, and a willingness to listen and grow.

Business

Understanding the changes in the business world doesn't require you to look much farther than your phone, your computer, or your watch. When Steve Jobs launched Apple computer, he didn't have a Business degree; he had a vision of what computers could do. Over time, his business skills grew, but the legacy he leaves is more one of inspired thinker than disciplined businessman – and in leaving that legacy, he's opened the doors of business to people from all walks of like, who have degrees in all kinds of fields.

This isn't to say that the scientist who wants to go into business on her own wouldn't do well to take a couple of Business classes as electives, or the environmental studies major who wants to make social media videos shouldn't have a best friend who knows a few things about marketing. But changes in the way products are made and sold suggest that the traditional days are over when the inspired inventor handed everything over to the Business major, and stayed in the lab to develop more inventions. Innovators from all backgrounds are picking up what they need to know about business in online classes and college electives and running their own companies, often with great success.

As you think about the major you'd like to pursue, take some time to consider how that major is shared, distributed, or marketed to the rest of the world. What products are made as a result of understanding this major? What companies exist because of it? What events are attended, promoted, and talked about on social media that exist only because of this major? In answering this question, you're looking at the business side of the major – and if you don't see it, you're just looking in the wrong place.

Entrepreneurship

Closely related to the world of business, more and more people are looking to the world of self-employment to make a living. With a strong background in their field, clear communication skills, and the discipline to offer unique services and promote them, many college graduates are finding ways to produce, promote, and distribute products and concepts on their own, making the world a better place to live in along the way.

While business and entrepreneurship are closely related, it's important to remember that being your own boss usually requires much more discipline and planning than being part of a business team. It's always important to carry your own weight in the business world, but when you're in business for yourself, you are the business – and that's a difference not everyone wants to live with. Most majors have plenty of room for independent go-getters to create a new market; it's just as important to make sure you'll always be eager to get going.

Government

With millions of people pulling their paychecks from the United States government, there's a very good chance at least a few thousand of them are getting paid to do something that relates to the major you want to pursue. While some of them are more obvious than others (like political science and nuclear energy), a closer look will reveal government connections to the field you're in. Studying Economics? Who do you think prepares the budget and analyzes it every year? Thinking about environmental science? The federal government has to maintain vast acres of forests west of the Rockies. Love history? Every federal museum has to have historians to maintain the accuracy of the displays, and the State Department has historians and cultural experts on every country in the world on staff.

Finding a perfect match between your major and a government job may take a while, but the steps couldn't be easier. To get some idea of the areas of government where you could land, start with the web pages of the career service sites mentioned in the start of this chapter. Many of these sites will discuss the kind of government jobs – federal, state, and local – available to people with your academic background.[9]

While state and local job postings can usually be found with an online search for "Job postings for the state of _____". Again, finding the right match for a unique major may take a while; then again, you may be amazed at the number of government jobs where someone who holds a degree in anything is qualified.

Technology

Much like business, the days of leaving anything having to do with technology to the code writers is over. Sure, you can make very good money learning code (no matter what degree you hold), but there are a number of tech fields looking for content experts to make sure the subject matter of websites, apps, and social media discussions is factually correct. Field experts will still turn it over to the tech crew to make the words and images look pretty, but those holding the degrees in other fields are the ones who make sure the words and images make sense.

Just as the tech world needs experts in other fields to make sure the information is correct, experts in these same fields are needed to make sure the technology is used in the right way where other field experts apply what they know. Many historians need to keep accurate records of events, but some historians need to keep track of the data collection tools used to record the events themselves. Ornithologists taking samples of fallen bird feathers have to use proper techniques to categorize their findings in the field, but those findings have to be

---

[9]Finding a specific job is as easy as going to https://www.usajobs.gov/ for federal work

catalogued the right way at the research center in order for the results to benefit the public at large. Starting with a degree in a specific field, combined with some training in technology as elective classes or a double major, allows the student to understand both the subject matter and the means communicating the subject matter – and that can be an awesome combination.

Avocation, or Hobby

There are a number of people who start out in their field with great enthusiasm, only to realize after a few years (or less) that, while they loved studying this subject in college, there's just no way they can make a living with the job options this field exists. Many of these people will then develop a two-part career and major interest, where part of their life is devoted to working hard at a job that meets their needs, while another part is devoted to studying something they love that can't pay the bills. This is why adults with kids of their own still play in rock bands on weekends; it's why people with factory jobs volunteer their weekends counting deer or identifying birds; it's why product salespeople offer to help the needy prepare their taxes.

Many people are fortunate enough to do something they love for a living, but when the realities of the job market or the economic needs of the individual prevent that from happening, there are still ways to follow the passion developed by your college major and make sure the rent gets paid. Looking around long and hard at all of the career options of a given major is the best way to make sure you don't have to choose between making ends meet and keeping a job you can't live without. It's also the best way to keep happy when that choice has to be made, knowing you've done everything you can to avoid that choice, and understanding how to keep the interest you developed in college alive and well.

More Resources

For a list of additional resources visit:
http://www.thebestschools.org/savvy-students/chapter-resources/

Career Trends: Where the Jobs Are

The Big Picture

Finding the growing occupations in the job market is a little more complicated than most people realize. While the federal government has an easy-to-find list of the careers where there are lots of job openings, not all of those careers offer the kind of salary many young people dream of, or are in the fields that are of interest to some people. A look at some additional resources that address higher-paying job fields that have openings shows that students considering these careers need to be prepared to take on a higher level of risk in most of these jobs, where bigger financial success is available, but not guaranteed. After looking a little closer at the job openings for the widely-discussed STEM fields, we look at the best way to prepare for a career in the business world, and find there are two answers. We then take a brief tour of the United States, assessing the differences in the job markets in several major cities, and provide some guidelines for students to complete a search for "hot" jobs in their field. Since jobs in popular or emerging fields come with their own challenges, we finish this chapter with a summary of the advantages and disadvantages of working in a popular or emerging field, along with some advice on how to evaluate the reasons why some field have a traditionally high amount of turnover, and what to do to make sure you don't become another employee who comes and goes quickly in any given field.

One of the most challenging parts of choosing a career involves understanding the future of that career – what are the current opportunities to work in that field, are those jobs going to be here in 10 or 20 years, does this career offer opportunities for promotions and raises, will there be more jobs available in this field in the future, and will this career be changing anytime soon?

These aren't easy questions to answer. Ten years ago, workers in auto assembly plants were sure they would have secure jobs for years to come. As a result of growing changes in technology and a decline in the economy, those jobs disappeared by the thousands. In this same time period, the idea of making a living producing videos and placing them on social media websites seemed like a dream. Ten years later, video bloggers have very loyal followers, and some are making enough money to live incredible lifestyles, all in their ability to produce a 7 minute video on a regular basis.

Year after year, when people ask futurists about the jobs that will soon be popular, the answer is always the same – five years from now, all of the high demand jobs will be ones that don't even exist now. There's a reason why this is always the answer to this question, and we'll talk about that. We'll also talk about how it's possible to follow your passion, even if you're not sure about the job prospects in your field.

But first, let's talk about the hot jobs.

Trends in Employment

When people ask about "hot" jobs, they usually want to know which fields are hiring more workers than they currently have. Using that definition, it's best to turn to the US Department of Labor, which offers a very clear, data-based picture of hiring trends. Their current top 10 includes:[1]

- Health-care related jobs (physical and occupational therapy assistants, home health aides, genetic counselors, sonographers, personal care aides, industrial psychologists)
- Skilled trades (brick mason assistants, mechanical insulation workers)
- Translators

Many people look at this list and realize two things. First, they realize it makes sense; as America's Baby Boomers move towards (and beyond) retirement, their healthcare needs are only going to increase. This is one of the main reasons why seven of the ten job fields that are growing are in health care.

The second thing many people realize when looking at this list is that, as a rule, these jobs don't pay very well. Of these ten growing jobs, only one (industrial psychologist) breaks far away from the me-

---

[1] http://blog.dol.gov/2015/03/15/the-10-fastest-growing-jobs/

dian household income in the United States – so, unless you plan on going into psychology, none of these growing jobs are going to make you rich.

If the lack of wealth in this list disappoints you, it may be time to look at the idea of "hot" jobs with an additional consideration – what job sectors are growing that offer great salaries? This gets a little trickier, since "good pay" is something everyone has a different definition for. For example, Business Insider offers their list of high-paying hot jobs to include software developer, market research analyst, and physical therapist – but their definition of "high paying" is more than $22 per hour, or about $44,000 per year.[2] Using that definition, more than half of the jobs identified on the Department of Labor site would also be considered high paying.

OK, you're thinking – but what about careers where you can make amazing money? Where are the growth opportunities there? LinkedIn offers these ten suggestions for fields where there is room to make at least $100,000 a year:[3]

- Technology (software and web development)
- Business (investment banker, business consultant, sales, entrepreneur)
- Author
- Speaker
- Engineer
- Orthodontist

As we look at this list, it's important to understand that many of these fields include something the careers on the other lists don't include – a high level of risk. There's no doubt that some authors and public speakers can make a great deal of money if they write a bestseller or speak on a popular topic, but for every author that makes it big, there are dozens who are self-publishing just to make a living. The same is true for entrepreneurs and web designers. A popular web page can lead to millions in ads and sales, but for every one that gets to that level, hundreds will get less than a dozen hits a day.

---

[2]http://www.businessinsider.com/12-fast-growing-high-paying-jobs-in-2014-2013-12

[3]https://www.linkedin.com/pulse/20140531085215-71158614-if-i-were-22-10-jobs-that-can-make-you-rich-before-30

As we look at growing job prospects for other majors, it comes as no surprise that engineering and computer-related jobs dominate the best jobs to get in the sciences – but some surprises round out the list of the top ten. In assessing the top ten STEM fields, Monster.com includes careers in Mathematics, Petroleum Technology, and Marine Sciences.[4] Taken together, these growing sectors suggest that any student pursuing a STEM major will be able to translate their studies into a career in a growing field that is well-paying, if not high-paying. That's something to consider in making plans on what college to attend, and how to finance it.

As much as STEM careers are discussed in the media, there's also good news for students interested in the arts and humanities. Study.com lists 25 top careers for humanities majors, and while most of them don't get to the high end of the salary scale, most of them dispel the idea that humanities majors are going to end up broke for all of their lives.[5] Their list includes:

- Translators (a Top 10 choice from the US Department of Labor)
- Writer (foreign correspondent, linguist, editor, technical writer)
- Advertising (Advertising Sales Agent, Public Relations Manager, Advertising Manager)
- FBI Agent

One area Study.com doesn't discuss is the opportunities in business that are wide open for Humanities majors. This is a debate that's been going on for many, many years. Are companies better off hiring people with Business degrees, where they have been trained to run any and all kinds of businesses, or are they better off hiring Humanities majors, who have studied the great ideas of the world, and can apply them to any setting, including the business world?

There isn't any data to show the "best" answer here, but past practice would suggest every company needs a mix of both. Studies may show that many CEOs come from liberal arts schools, but for every successful company run by a big thinker, there's a financial officer who's making the place turn a tidy profit, thanks to the training they received in business school. This means there's plenty of room for

---

[4]http://www.monster.com/career-start/a/top-10-most-valuable-STEM-majors-and-careers

[5]http://study.com/articles/25_Great_Jobs_for_Humanities_Majors.html

both Business and Humanities majors in the business world, a combination that has stood the test of time.

Trends by Geographic Region

In addition to looking for the best job prospects by major or career, many students are eager to know what fields are open based on the location of the job. More and more students are looking beyond their local boundaries, interested in starting fresh lives in a new part of the country, if not the world. We'll limit our discussion to the United States, and take a look at selected markets throughout the country. This information comes from the Bureau of Labor Statistics, which identifies hot jobs by the percentage of growth – so that doesn't always mean the greatest number of jobs are in these fields, but it does mean the rate of increase is highest in these fields.

New York
The Big Apple reflects national growth in medical areas, including physical therapist aides and industrial psychologists, and the nation's needs for technology specialists is also reflected in the country's largest city. Local additions to the strong jobs list includes casino workers, insulation workers, convention and event planners, and statisticians. Cooks are also included in the New York list, a reminder of the upcoming national shortage of chefs that's expected to hit the country in the next couple of years.

Washington, DC
The job market in our nation's capital largely reflects the job market in New York, except for the need for casino workers, since Washington does not have a strong casino presence. Instead, workers in the DC area would do well to focus on careers in personal finance and in security, where the need for more workers will be greatest by numbers. Two interesting categories on this list also includes musicians and athletes. While the number of jobs in these areas isn't big, the fact that these careers are appearing on a hot list is noteworthy. Given the competitive nature of these fields, this need for openings is good news, to be sure.

Atlanta

The hot spot of the South has a remarkable need for healthcare workers of all types. While some health fields are represented on the national report, nearly every top spot in the Georgia report is health care related, setting it apart from the national norms. The only exceptions are business agents for artists and athletes (a big money field), and interpreters. Other than that, the medical field is bursting at the seams.

Detroit

Detroit is included in this list because it has emerged from bankruptcy to find itself as a destination hot spot for young people, especially artists. Statewide, the national need for healthcare workers is reflected, but there is also a real need for workers in the skilled trades, including welders and brick masons. Engineers of different kinds are also needed in many areas, but not in the automotive area, where the Motor City never seems to run out of designers that want to make better cars.

Chicago

Chicago mirrors Atlanta in its need for healthcare workers and translators. The need for anything in technology or business is remarkably small in Illinois, with Numeric Machine operators making the list, as well as analysts, but that's about it. Chicago will also be in need of convention and event planners.

San Francisco and Los Angeles

The home of the technology boon reports a remarkable need for construction workers, including marble setters, terrazzo workers, insulation workers, and stone masons. Two fields not found on many other reports that are booming in California are Foresters and Anthropologists, where the anticipated job growth is above 40% in both fields. The largest growing field in California is also not found in many other states, as California expects a 65% growth in its need for economists.

How to Look for Trends in Your Field

If we look at all of these reports as a group, there seems to be a little bit of good news for everyone. The fastest growing area seems to be healthcare, a trend that started over fifteen years ago, and continues to expand as America gets older. From personal aides to industrial psychologists, these openings offer a wide range of salaries, and require everything from a high school diploma to advanced training at the doctorate level. If you're looking for an area where your employment will be readily available and the work demands are steady, healthcare is the go-to field for the foreseeable future.

If you're interested in a career with a little more risk and the possibility of a little more reward, the fields where the room is greatest seem to be writing, speaking, and business – specifically, entrepreneurism. This last trend is also one that's been with us for a very long time, and that's good; it shows us that the spirit of American individualism is alive and well, and still getting recognized in the marketplace. If you can manage the ups and downs of a career that is more than nine-to-five and the paychecks aren't consistent, these fields will work for you nicely. Best of all, most of them allow you to major in whatever you like, then learn the skills necessary to make a handsome living talking, writing, or manufacturing what you love.

Despite the across-the-board good news these reports bring, there are some who are hoping for more specific data about their specialty. This information isn't always readily available, and when it is, the sources can sometimes be limited by geographic region, or based on data that is incomplete. Still, data is data; if you're interested in finding out about a specific field, try these sources:

Complete an online search

Running a search using the phrase "hot jobs in Biology" isn't likely to get you much information, since most of the articles a search like this digs up are articles about trends in general employment, and not current issues in Biology. Using different combinations, like "Biology jobs" or "careers in Biology" may end up giving you many articles about all careers in Biology, but you'll likely also get an article or two that tells you where to find the growth in Biology careers.

Talk with an instructor

We've already encouraged you to talk with a college instructor about general career prospects in a given field, and the same advice holds when looking for information on current hiring trends and areas of job growth. Since college professors have to conduct research, they're often exposed to leaders in the businesses, private foundations, and government agencies associated with your field. That's an awful lot of connections to an awful lot of data about jobs. Make the most of it.

Talk with the local Chamber of Commerce

If you're looking for local advice on the jobs that are in demand, your local Chamber can be your best friend. The workers at the Chamber are paid to know the strengths and weaknesses of the local economy, and that includes a solid understanding of the job market. If you're heading to a new town, or looking for a place where you can get off to a solid start in your career, a call to the Chamber can give you the information you need.

Look on professional websites

Just like you turn to the Society of Engineers to find out what you can do with a degree in engineering, so you turn to the same resources to find out where those jobs are, and what the jobs of the future look like in that field. Not every page will offer detailed information, but it's a great place to start.

The Plusses and Minuses of Landing a "Hot" Job

At first, it makes perfect sense to choose a career in a field where the demand is high and the need is great. But every job has its plusses and minuses, even if they're new, and even if they're popular. Here are some considerations as you consider if a growing job is for you:

Greater geographic mobility

More jobs usually means more places where you can work, not just in your home town, but in many towns. Some trends are local, but many have an impact felt from coast to coast – and that can be a big plus when you're young and looking for a place to call your own.

Greater upward mobility

Many of the emerging careers will be requiring more managers and administrators, and those positions are typically filled by line workers who know the field inside and out. If a field is growing fast, you may find yourself moving up fast – and that can be a good thing.

Greater innovation
Fields that have high needs usually have to find new ways to meet that need, which means that field needs people who think creatively and can solve problems others can't see. This is especially true in health care, where employee shortages seem to always occur. Finding a way to produce quality health care with less staff that still has a personalized touch is arguable the biggest task for the workforce of the future, and that's an exciting idea.

High risk/high reward
Not every field that needs more workers is brand new, but many of the emerging fields are trying to create new markets, or capture new markets. That means the pace of growth will be fast, and some ideas will work, but some won't. Those that do will be highly rewarded, and those that don't will soon be forgotten. Riding that wave isn't for everyone, and it's something to consider before taking the plunge into new waters.

Greater possibility for change
Innovation is usually seen as a good thing, but some people who like the "old ways" sometimes feel left behind when change comes their way – especially if it's change they don't like, or don't understand. If flexibility isn't one of your strengths, working in a growing field may not be for you. Think about that carefully.

Need for ongoing professional development
Every field offers training to keep their employees on top of the current trends of the profession. That's especially true in a field where the trends are changing every year – or every month. It will be important to be a good student when you enter an emerging field. Keep that in mind as you sort out your career interests.

High turnover
An emerging field often means a number of start-up companies, and that means some will get bought out by others, even if they're a success. If you're going to begin a career in one of these fields, be sure to understand the complete range of benefits available to you, especially stock options and buy-out language. These often won't come into play unless the company is taken over or merges, but once that

happens, it's too late to change the rules of the game. The time to do that is now, so make sure you understand what could happen – and pay close attention to talk about mergers and sell-offs as you complete your daily work.

Another factor to consider in going into a field with high turnover is to look closely for the reasons why so many people take a position in this field, but then leave just as quickly. A long standing example of this is in the field of teaching, where workers train for five years, only to leave the profession after only five to eight years of work, according to different studies. Of course, there may be different reasons why so many people leave teaching after such a brief time, but there may also be something more to working in this field than the training suggests. If you're looking to join a field where people come and go quickly, be sure to talk to people in that profession to get the inside story on what it takes to be successful in that field. Job shadowing or interning may help you understand this as well, so it's always a good idea to include those experiences in your training for the field.

More Resources

For a list of additional resources visit:
http://www.thebestschools.org/savvy-students/chapter-resources/

Writing an Effective Résumé

The Big Picture

The key to writing an effective résumé is to understand that the résumé needs to tell the reader – your potential employer – everything they want to know about you. That may not be the same as everything you want to tell them about yourself, so it's important to focus on your audience as you put your résumé together. This is also true when deciding which of the three résumé types to use, depending partially on the job, but depending more on your work experience. The plusses and minuses of digital résumés are discussed, and the major sections of the résumé are reviewed to make sure the applicant is presenting themselves with the right mix of professionalism and creativity, designed to make them stand out from the other applicants in just the right way. This same balance of professionalism and creativity is important to achieve in choosing the type face and formatting of the résumé, as well as the cover letter, where the applicant can go into more detail of their experience and interest in the position, all with the goal in mind of securing an interview for the position.

Once you've found the career you want to pursue or the college you'd like to apply to, it's time to take the steps to get that job or receive that acceptance letter – and that usually involves a résumé. To many people, putting a résumé together can be pretty intimidating; how can you summarize your life in one page in a way that convinces the person reading it that they want you above all the other applicants? By using a few tried-and-true guidelines and mixing them with a little bit of creativity, you'll see how easy it is to put together a statement that will leave the reader wanting to know more – and that's what will lead to an interview.

Purpose of a Résumé

One of the reasons people have such a hard time writing a résumé is that they don't understand what a résumé is for. That's no small thing, since a résumé can only be effective if you know how to use it. It's like if you tried to use your music app to order a pizza online; you'd only end up frustrated and no closer to your goal than when you started.

The reason for this confusion is that too many people who have told you what a résumé is for are wrong. The purpose of a résumé is to give someone the information they want to know about you. It isn't designed to tell the reader everything about your life, or your personal life, or your school life, or your professional life – it's only supposed to tell them just what they want to know.

This means the first step towards writing an effective résumé is understanding what the reader wants to know, and how to best communicate that to them. In some cases, this is pretty easy to figure out, since they will be nice enough to tell you in the job posting or the application.

> "Please submit a résumé with your educational experience, job experience, and any skills related to your work in social media."

These instructions are pretty clear, so you know exactly what to include. The last line may be a little confusing – do they just want to know what social media sites you use, or do they want to know the ones you're familiar with, or do they want to know you know how to post a picture to Facebook? The job description can help clear this up, but it's likely that if you tell them you use Facebook, they'll know you know how to use most of its major functions.

> "Please submit a résumé with any additional experiences you were not able to include on the application."

At first, these instructions may seem a little less specific, but they offer a clue in what to include by sending you to the application you also have to submit. A quick look at that form gives you some idea of what to do with your résumé. If you've run out of space on the application to list your job experiences, education, hobbies, or whatever else they've asked you to include, the résumé is the place to continue those lists and descriptions.

> "Please include a cover letter and résumé."

OK – this isn't too much help. Now you're on your own, so it will be helpful to know what kind of résumé to use, keeping in mind that your goal is to tell them everything they want to know about you, and nothing more.

Employment Résumés

It helps to think of the résumé as a tool, and just like there are different kinds of tools for different kinds of jobs, there are different kinds of résumés for different kinds of jobs. ISeek.com provides a nice summary of the three traditional kinds of résumés.[1] Each one includes basic information like your contact information, education, hobbies, and references, but they vary in the way your work experience is presented.

Chronological résumé
The chronological résumé is the kind most people think of when putting a résumé together. It lists each job you've had, starting with the most recent job, and going backwards in time, or in reverse chronological order. With each job, you include a brief description of what you did on that job. You usually don't include why you left that position; if that is of interest to the employer, they'll either ask you that on a related job application, or discuss it with you in an interview.

Functional résumé
The functional résumé doesn't list the jobs that you've had. Instead, you list and describe the skills and projects you've worked on, in order to give the employer an idea of the talents you have, the kinds of work experiences you've had, and the results of the work you've done.

As ISeek.com points out, using this kind of résumé comes with some degree of risk. Most people use a functional résumé when they don't have a great deal of job experience, or if they haven't held any one job for a long period of time. Since a functional résumé doesn't list the dates of your employment, or even your employers, it's one way to focus on what you can bring to the job as a result of your life experiences, including volunteer work.

---

[1] http://www.iseek.org/jobs/ résumécharts.html

On the other hand, without some sense of where you've worked and how long you stayed there, employers often read the functional résumé with the understanding that you either have very little work experience, or that you didn't stay at any one job for very long. That might not matter to an employer who is looking for someone to work on a project for a short period of time, or for a company looking to hire you for a few months during a busy period. But a company looking for a longer-term commitment is likely to prefer a chronological résumé.

Combination résumé

If you think the employer wants a chronological résumé, but your work experience is better suited for using the functional résumé format, think about using the combination résumé, which lists both the skills you have and your work history. In many ways, this format is the best of both worlds, since it shows the reader both where you've worked and what skills you have. The only challenge with this format is that it often leads to a two-page résumé, where your work experience ends up on the second page. Since most employers either require or are used to seeing only one-page résumés, this makes using this format a challenge; but if the job requires a unique set of detailed skills, this still might be the best approach, even if the résumé extends to a second page.

Educational Résumés

If you're applying for admission to college, some colleges will either require a résumé, or give you the option of submitting one to supplement the information you've given them on the application. While this is more common for students who are applying for Masters or Doctoral programs, there are a few colleges that ask for a résumé as part of an undergraduate application to admission.

An educational résumé usually includes the same basic content as a chronological résumé – contact information, education, and employment history, which in this case can include volunteer or community service work. In addition, an educational résumé can include involvement in extracurricular activities, and awards and recognition. An educational résumé usually doesn't include references, since most admission applications also ask for letters of recommendation. Educational résumés can also include a summary of any research the student has completed. Students applying to graduate school are more likely to have research experience, but if a high school student has been fortunate enough to have this opportunity, including it in the résumé can really separate you from the other applicants.

Since most students don't have extensive work experience, the combination format of a job résumé might be the best choice for your educational résumé. This allows you to emphasize the skills you've learned through your volunteer and leadership experiences in school, as well as your work history.[2]

The Curriculum Vitae

As you're putting together your educational résumé, you may run across a request to "submit either a résumé or a CV." CV is an abbreviation for **curriculum vitae**, which is Latin for "course of life." The biggest difference between the two is that a résumé is a brief summary of the information you're providing, while a CV offers much more detail about the skills and experiences you've had. Since CVs tend to be asked for with higher executive positions, or with some graduate school applications, we won't go into detail about the CV here – just know that it's a longer alternative to a résumé that you should only use if the choice is offered to you, and if you have extensive work or research experience that just can't fit into one page.[3]

Digital Résumés

It should come as no surprise that technology had created some alternatives to the traditional one-page, hard copy résumé, and many of these alternatives are, well, cool. One of the big plusses of most digital résumés is that they include charts and other visuals that bring your work and educational histories to life in a way words can't. With the use of graphs and videos, these formats can also be faster to create, since many of them just require you to download the information you already have on a professional social media site, like LinkedIn.[4]

---

[2] A nice example of this can be found at livecareer (http://www.livecareer.com/ résumé-examples/education)

[3] If you're curious, you can see an example of a curriculum vitae on theundercoverrecruiter.com (http://theundercoverrecruiter.com/cv-vs-résumé-difference-and-when-use-which/).

[4] Some examples of these digital résumés can be found on themuse.com (https://www.themuse.com/advice/5-digital-tools-that-will-make-your-résumé-infinitely-more-beautiful).

Of course, one of the considerations you'll need to make before submitting a digital résumé is how it will be received by the reader. You may think your digital résumé is just amazing, but if the reader is unfamiliar with digital résumés, doesn't know how to read one, or thinks this is just a clever way for you to send a two-page résumé when they've asked you to limit your résumé to one page, the goal of having a résumé is defeated, and you'd be better off going old school instead. Advertising firms, tech companies, and art schools may see digital résumés as great ways to get to know you, but the rest of the world may not see it that way. Unless the job posting or application says otherwise, call human resources and ask them if they accept digital résumés. If there's any doubt, stick with the traditional one-page hard copy, and be prepared to wow them with a couple of digital handouts in your interview.

Content of a Résumé

While we've discussed parts of the résumé when we talked about the kinds of résumé, it's a good idea to do a quick review, including some tips on résumé basics that can make the difference between getting to the next round and being placed in the long file of applicants that may be considered later.

Contact Information
You would think nothing could go wrong with the part of the résumé that includes your name, address, telephone, and email address, right? But as ISeek.com points out, there are three things to consider here that can set you apart from the other applicants in a hurry—but not in a good way.

First, take a look at your email address. If it's the one you've been using since middle school, it might be time to create a new account that's separate from your personal email. This is especially true if your personal email address is crazyskateboarder@dude.com. Advertising agencies and employers that work with creative people might admire a clever email address, but they are also businesses, so they'll be OK with something as simple as your name. Play it safe for now, and try that.

Second, call your own phone number, and listen to your outgoing voice mail message. Can you understand what you're saying? Is the tone professional and welcoming, or did you record this the day you got your phone, and you decided to try and be funny? Again, there will be time for them to get to know your funny side in the interview. Listen to the image you're portraying, and consider re-recording.

Finally, take a moment to look at your digital footprint. Putting your contact information for LinkedIn, Twitter, or other social media is a good idea only if the employer will be impressed in a positive way by what they see when they look at your account. If you haven't updated the information, or if it's more personal than anything else, consider leaving that information off the contact portion of your résumé. In addition, think about taking down old social media accounts completely, especially if the content is questionable. Sure, sharing pictures from homecoming seemed like a great idea the day after, but those are now out there for employers and colleges to see – and that might be too much information too soon.

Objective

This is a one sentence statement of what you're looking for. "To share my creative talents in web design and communication with a company committed to improving the quality of online content." A successful objective statement includes what you have to offer, and where you'd like to offer it, all in one tidy sentence – and since it's just one sentence, that means you may spend a long time making sure this sentence is accurate, thorough, and well written.

Summary

Many people worry that a résumé doesn't offer them the chance to give any details about themselves, or about their life experiences. The summary statement gives you that chance, by trying to answer the question "What have you done in your life that relates to the job you're applying for?" Again, it's important to keep in mind that you aren't telling them everything about yourself; you're just telling them what they want to know so they can decide if you're the right person for the job, or for the college.[5]

Educational Experience

Nothing too fancy here – just the degree you earned, the name of the school that gave it to you, the year you received it, and if it came

---

[5]See http://www.iseek.org/jobs/ résumécontents.html for an example of this.

with any academic honors ("Diploma, Washington High School, 2015, *cum laude*"). Some older applicants may want to leave the year off, and that's OK. Including your GPA is fine on an educational résumé, but not required.

Skill Summary

If you're using the functional résumé or combination résumé format, you then list the skills you want the reader to know about. With a functional résumé, you have a little more space to go into detail about your skills ("Word processing, including work with Word 8.2, NotePad, Ituit, and WordStar"). With a combination résumé, you need to tighten things up a little bit ("Word processing on all widely used formats, spreadsheets, all popular e-mail software").

It's helpful to include a summary of the "soft skills" you've also used, if space allows, since qualities like teamwork, leadership, critical thinking, and empathic listening can be extras that will make the difference in getting an interview. Your best bet is to complete the résumé without listing these; if it's clear you have space to add them once the other essentials are there, go back and put them in the end of this section.

Work Experience

If you're using the chronological format or combination format, you include the job title you held, the name of the company, the city where you did the work, and the dates of employment. If you have room, include one or two sentences describing your work. Some people will just list these details ("Oversaw an office of eight staff"), while others will use a narrative ("My team of eight and I worked on every aspect of customer service.") Most employers see the narrative as more engaging, and that can make a difference.

If your work experience is limited, you may include related volunteer work, as long as you make it clear that you were a volunteer. This is especially important is you're using the combination format, since the primary reason you're listing volunteer experiences is to explain where you developed some of the skills you've listed in the skill summary.

Hobbies

No matter what format you use here, the key here is brevity.

See? That one line really got your attention – and that's the key with the hobby section. You only want to list as many hobbies as will fill one line. If you have more than that, pick the ones that you think will be of most interest to the reader. If you're a hunter, and you happen to know the employer is a hunter, list it. If you don't know who will be reading your résumé, list the hobbies that are of greatest interest to you.

Some people wonder if there are some hobbies that are best left off a résumé. This is a tough question, and is kind of up to you. It's certainly true that if you're applying for a traditional business position, listing "bagpipe playing" as a hobby may give you the kind of attention you don't want to get. On the other hand, if your hobbies and interests really mean a great deal to you, would you want to work for someone who doesn't at least respect your interests, even if they don't share them?

The other important part of this section is honesty. To go back to our example, if you know the employer is a hunter, and you **aren't** a hunter, **don't say that you are.** Not only do you run the risk of being considered a liar, it also avoids any kind of embarrassment in the interview, where the interviewer could decide to get to know you by talking about hunting. If you don't have any hobbies, or don't want to talk about them, leave this section off the résumé. Most employers consider this section optional, so if it isn't on your résumé, they won't miss it.

References

The growing trend today is to leave references off a résumé completely. There was a time when references were listed, including their contact information; that trend then changed, where this section simply stated "Available upon request." Now, employers assume you'll be able to give them the names of three references if they ask for them, and if you make it to the interview round – so you really shouldn't have a reference section at all.

If this news disappoints you, it shouldn't. The fact that your résumé won't have someone's contact information on it for all the world to see is probably good news for your references, who really don't need more people to have their email address for no particular reason. In addition, the absence of references on your résumé allows you to custom tailor the references you give each employer or college, depending on the nature of the work, or the college you're applying to. If you're applying to become an office worker, you'd want to include a different set of references than if you're applying to become a supervisor of office workers – and that's a different set of references than if you're applying to become a supervisor of office workers who write computer code. If the idea of not being able to include the name of your famous employer on a résumé is a downer, don't worry – you can dazzle the reader when they ask for references during the interview.

Appearance

It may seem strange, but the appearance of your résumé is just as important as the content and the format. It's easy to think that hundreds of one-page summaries of the lives of applicants would all look the same after a while, and you're right – too often, they do. This means the presentation of your information – the typeface you choose, the colors you print it in, the formatting of the information, and even the quality of the paper it's printed on – can make the difference in getting to the next step of the selection process.

There are two key components to consider as you put the format of your résumé together. First, it's usually a good idea not to use the format that automatically comes with any résumé website or information program you're using. To begin with, many of these formats are just unattractive; many of them use fonts that are too small, or too big, and many others don't use underlining, bold face, or section headers in ways that are attractive. In addition, if all you're doing is using the automatic format, what do you think the thousands of other users of that program are doing – and as a result, how much will your résumé stand out from theirs? It may take some extra time and expense, but putting together a uniquely formatted résumé can make a big difference.

The second component to consider is the creativity component of a résumé. If the "traditional" résumé is one page, are there times when it's OK for yours to be two pages – or can you do something creative like print on two sides of one page, or use both sides of the page by folding the résumé into a booklet?

The current thought regarding résumés is to proceed with caution. To begin with, many employers and colleges are requesting online résumés, or submissions of résumés as attachments to e-mails. This rules out doing anything creative with folding the paper. In addition, many other employers are simply asking you to submit your résumé information through an online résumé program, where (sadly) everyone's information has the same format. Finally, since you usually don't know who is going to read your résumé, doing something widely creative runs the risk of offending someone who takes a traditional approach to résumés, who will take one look at your "unusual" format, and decide not to interview you on that basis alone.

This isn't to say that some creativity is out of the question, especially if you're applying for a job in a field where creativity is seen as a must in any employee, or to a college where creativity is part of what you're going to study. Still, there needs to be a balance between creativity and professionalism. Take a look at the formatting samples by looking at the images of a Web search for résumé formats, and consider the right balance of personal expression and the format that will most likely get you an interview.

Cover letters

The other opportunity to add to the brevity of your résumé is in your cover letter. While it also has to be brief – a cover letter is never more than one page – the cover letter has traditionally been seen as the place where the applicant can show a little more of their personality, provide more detail about their life and work experiences, and talk more about why this position is of interest to them. Since a résumé for a college application is already accompanied by other information, a cover letter isn't used when submitting information to a college.

There's a traditional format to a cover letter, and it's wise to follow it if you're applying for a position in a large company, since the first paragraph typically indicates what position you're applying for. It's important to make this clear to a large organization, since you want to make sure you'll be considered for the right position, and more than one might be available in a bigger company. The second paragraph offers some insights into why you're interested in the position, and what you might have to offer the company, and the third paragraph invites them to contact you if you can provide more information to support your application for the job, and gently urges them to give you an interview.[6] Just as there are ways to create résumé formats with the goal of setting yourself apart from others, there are also ways to put together a cover letter to achieve the same goal. One of the most widely used, and often successful, techniques is to jump right in and talk about your interest in the position, and use the introductory language later. "Acme Incorporated is known throughout the world as a leader in technology development, and the need for leadership in cybersecurity has never been greater" is a strong opening sentence that gets the attention of the reader, and makes known the reason for your interest in the job right away. Following that up with a brief summary of the challenges facing the cybersecurity industry, you can then follow that up in a second paragraph with something like "The experiences and skills I've had in cybersecurity line up perfectly with this need, and can help Acme reach its goals in this crucial area." After following this up with a brief summary of your skills, you conclude with "I look forward to discussing my qualifications with you for the position of Vice President of Security Development. A copy of my résumé is enclosed. Please let me know if I can provide any additional information."

To be sure, this approach isn't for everyone, especially if your experience and skill set for the available position is relatively small as someone just starting out in the world of employment. But the tone of this approach suggests this applicant has insights into the profession and a good amount of self-assurance that doesn't border on thinking they are the greatest person in the world. That kind of quiet confidence can make the right kind of difference in getting the attention of the employer, and move you towards the next important step – the interview.

More Resources

For a list of additional resources visit:
http://www.thebestschools.org/savvy-students/chapter-resources/

---

[6]For sample cover letters at
http://jobsearch.about.com/od/coverlettersamples/a/samplecovasst.htm.

GIVING A SUCCESSFUL INTERVIEW

The Big Picture

A well-constructed résumé can take you to the next step, which is usually an interview. In most cases, the content of a college application interview and a first job interview is very similar, keeping in mind that many colleges don't require interviews, while nearly every job requires some kind of interview as a condition of employment.

A key to a successful interview is how you present yourself, and that involves preparation in everything from the voice mail message you have on the phone line you give the interviewer, to the research you complete on the college or company before you interview, to the review you make of the information you've already provided the college or interview, to what you wear that day and when you arrive for the interview. You can expect specific kinds of questions to be asked during the interview, making it easier to prepare for. You'll also have the chance to ask questions of the interviewer, and you should be well prepared to present those. Some job interviews will lead to a second interview that is remarkably similar to the first round, but with a different group of people. If you're invited back for another interview, you should be prepared at any time to discuss salary and conditions of employment, since a job offer could come at any time before, during, or after the second interview.

Congratulations! You've put together an application and résumé that stood apart from the others enough to get you an interview for the college of your choice or the job of your dreams. But now that you're going to talk with someone in person, you're starting to feel a little nervous. It's one thing to find the right type font, because no one sees all the bad ones you selected before finding the right one. With interviews, there's plenty of time to practice, but only one chance to get it right, so let's review the key elements of an interview that will get you to the next step.

College Interviews

Whether it's for admission to college, to a special program, or for a college scholarship, there just aren't as many colleges requiring interviews for all applicants, and even fewer that will grant an interview to a student who asks for one. Part of this has to do with the growing number of students applying to top colleges; it's getting to the point where it's nearly impossible to talk with all of them and still make decisions on all applications in a timely fashion. If your college doesn't give interviews, that means it's all the more important to make sure your application is well put together, and says everything you need to say about yourself.

If your college does grant interviews, they are usually required of all applicants, and they come in a variety of ways. A limited number of interviews are often available on the college's campus, with someone from the admissions office, while other interviews will occur closer to where you live, and will be conducted by one of the alumni of the school, or someone who graduated from the college.

Some students are convinced that it's better to have an interview on-campus, and, in a way, they're right – but in a way, they aren't. Many colleges that interview also consider the student's **demonstrated interest in the college** as part of the decision process. If one student has submitted an application and visited the college campus, as well as talked with the admissions officer when they came to visit the applicant's high school, that student could hold a big advantage over a student who just applied to the college, and did nothing else. Why? Because the first student is showing more interest in the college by learning more about it in important ways, and using that information to make sure the fit is right between the student and the college. Since an on-campus interview means the student has to go to campus to participate, this is one way of showing you really think that college would be a good place for you to be.

On the other hand, just going to campus doesn't guarantee that what you say in the interview will be seen as more interesting, important, or successful than the student who is interviewed by a graduate of the college, or interviewed by the admissions office online, or by phone. Demonstrated interest is one category some colleges use in the selection process, but that's separate from the interview. As a result, the content of the interview will be judged in the same way as any other required interview – it will be based on how you present yourself, how you answer the questions, and the questions you ask.

Presenting yourself

No matter where your interview is held, you begin to make an impression the moment you're contacted to set up a time for the interview. Since you will likely be in class when that first call comes in, you want to make sure the voice mail message on your phone is clear and welcoming, and that you're checking your voice mail regularly to see if the interviewer has called. Once you get that message, try to call back as soon as you can. Most alumni interviewers are volunteers with limited time, and they may end up scheduling a number of interviews for the same day. If you wait too long to call back, your interview may be delayed, and that could have an impact on your application – or on the impression you leave with the interviewer, who may be wondering if you really care about going to their college, since you're taking your time to get back with them.

In setting up a time and a place to meet, it's best to try and meet when you're fresh and focused, so try and avoid evenings if possible – in fact, most students aim for interviews on weekends, or right after school, before team practices or homework. If you're getting an alumni interview, they will usually suggest you meet in their office (if they have one), a local coffee shop, or at your high school. If an admissions officer is going to interview you, they may have rented a meeting room at a local hotel. Confirm the date and time you'll be meeting, and ask them if you should bring any written materials with you.

Once the interview time is set, it's time to do a little homework on the school. If you've already submitted your application to the college, take the time to review your application, especially your essay answers. It's highly unlikely an alumni interviewer will have read your application, and it's very possible the admissions officer hasn't either, but this reminds you what you said to the college, and it helps you remember what you like about this college – and that's very important for the interview.

You'll also want to take a moment to come up with a couple of questions to ask your interviewer. It's pretty common for an interview to end with the opportunity for you to ask a question or two, and it's important that these questions show some kind of depth, and aren't questions that could easily be answered by reading the college's website. Choosing the right questions is especially important if your interviewer is part of the alumni of the college; they may love the college a great deal, but chances are, they might not know everything you want to know about the college's neuroscience program, or the job placement rate of the last graduating class.

In putting your questions together, you'll want to find a way to give the interviewer a chance to offer a mix of fact and their opinion when they answer. If the interviewer is one of the alumni, a great question to ask is "I'm thinking about majoring in (insert your major here.) How did you find your years as a student at this college prepared you for your career, both in and out of the classroom?" This question has a little bit of everything – information about you, a chance for the interviewer to discuss college programs, and room for them to share what they've done with the opportunities the college has provided them. Add one other question to this one, and you should be all set.[1]

The day of the interview

When the big day comes, you want to make sure you're well dressed for an interview. It's strongly advised that you set a time for the interview that doesn't require you to go there right after school, so you can have a chance to change clothes and freshen up. It's wise to plan on wearing something that is clean, wrinkle-free, and a little on the business side. This doesn't mean guys have to wear a suit, or even a tie, and girls certainly don't need to wear a dress (and shouldn't wear an evening gown, as one very overdressed student did). Still, this is the time to leave your jeans, leggings, low-cut tops, droopy pants, and belly shirts at home, no matter how "cool" you think the college is. The goal is to dress in a way that makes both you and your interviewer comfortable, and since you don't know their comfort level, it's wise to play it safe and be on the conservative side. No matter what you end up wearing, run a brush through your hair, brush your teeth, and if you're wearing shoes that can be polished, polish them the night before. You would be amazed what a different that will make all by itself.

You'll want to arrive to the interview about ten minutes before it's scheduled to start. If something happens where you're going to be late – or you're going to just get there in time – call the interviewer and let them know. Once you meet, say hello, tell them your name, and thank

---

[1] For more ideas on questions to ask, see http://www.hercampus.com/high-school/5-best-questions-ask-your-college-interviewer.

them for the chance to talk about a college you've learned a lot about. If you've brought them some written information – a copy of your résumé or your essays, for example – either give them to the interviewer right away, or set them on a table once you sit down. If you hold on to them during the interview, they will likely be a rolled-up mess, and that will leave an impression, but not a good one.

The questions the interviewer will ask will likely run something like this:

"Tell me about yourself."

The key with every question is to make sure it's the right length, but that's especially true with the first question. Interviewers know they're in for a long day if you answer this question with "Well, I was born in Detroit on June 22, 1999." With this question, and with every question, you want the answer to be more than just "Yes" or "No", but you also don't want to string together three answers that are all five minutes long. Since you're likely to be a little excited about the interview, keep your answers to two breaths. Once you're about to inhale for your third breath, it's time to stop answering that question.

"What do you like to do in your free time?"

Just like college essays, students are convinced there is a "right" answer to this question, and there is – tell them the truth. If you hang out with your friends, and you think that answer doesn't sound ambitious enough, start by telling the interviewer what you do with the rest of your day. "Well, I usually have team practice after school, and then I do homework, and I tutor for a couple of hours on Saturday – so once that's all done, catching up with my friends is something I look forward to."

"What interests you about our college?"

If this sounds like a remix of the "Why Us" essay question, it is – and since the interviewer probably hasn't read your answer, you can use most of it when answering this question. It's always wise to add a little new information to your answer, just in case they have read your essay, so be sure to have an additional idea to share with them – and since your essay most likely talked about academics, this extra piece can talk about the social life or some other part of the campus.

"Do you have any questions I can answer?"

Here's where your homework paid off. Be sure you commit your question to memory, and look the interviewer straight in the eye when you ask the questions. Maintain eye contact while they answer, and smile when they're finished answering.

As the interview ends, shake hands, thank them again for the chance to interview, and leave as quickly as you can. Once you're alone, make a couple of note of the highlights of the interview—what you think went well – and be sure you remember the interviewer's name...

After the interview

...because the day after the interview, you want to send a brief thank you note to the interviewer. To be honest, it's best if this comes in the format of a hand written note, on a nice card – that is a step that will really set you apart from others in a positive way. But it's likely that all you'll have is the interviewer's email address, so it's OK to send it that way instead.

The content of the note is simple. "Thank you again for the chance to talk with you about my interest in Southeastern Michigan. I really appreciated hearing about what the school means to you, and how it helped you advance your career in telecommunications."

After another sentence or two that includes either your thoughts on the interview, or any additional information they've asked you to provide, finish up by saying "Please let me know if I can provide any additional information, and thank you again for taking the time to meet with me."

Believe it or not, those seven sentences will put you much, much farther down the road of being a successful college applicant than most students, because most students don't bother to do this.

Job Interviews

The format of many traditional job interviews is identical to that used in college interviews, especially if the interview is with a smaller company, where the first interview is likely to be with just one person. In some cases, a first interview will be with several people from the company, including the person who will be your immediate supervisor; one or two of your potential co-workers; a representative from human resources; and one or two people from departments in the company that work with the department that will employ you.

Regardless of the number of people interviewing you, your preparation for the interview is very much the same as the steps taken for the college interview. Take a moment to review your résumé, cover letter, and any application you completed for the job. Review the company's Web presence by looking at their Web page (including the specific division you'll be working in, if it has a separate section). Type in the company's name as a general Web search to see what other information is online about the company, including any recent presence they may have had in the news. Use a reliable business site to get a sense of the company's value and representation in the business community, and use all of this information to develop a few questions you might ask at the end of your interview.

Be sure to arrive early for your interview. Since rush hour traffic may be a factor in getting to the interview site, be prepared to sit in your car or at a nearby coffee shop if you're more than ten minutes early, since you don't want to appear too eager to the company. In terms of what to wear, it's pretty tough to beat business wear when you're interviewing for a job. If the position you've applied for involves working outside, you may want to be more on the business casual side, and that's definitely true if the company has a reputation for being more casual – but don't wander too far down the casual road. Just like a college interview, you don't know the tastes of your interviewer, and when dealing with the unknown, it's always best to be a little on the dressy side.

After introducing yourself to your interviewer(s), you'll find many of the questions are similar to those asked in the college interview – tell us about yourself, what are your hobbies, what interests you in the position. In addition, you can expect to have to address these questions:

"What skills do you bring to this position that set you apart from other candidates?"

If this seems like a tough question to answer, it is, since you have absolutely no idea what set of skills the other candidates have. The best way to answer this question is to think about the skills and experiences you've had allow you to give something extra to the job, like an internship with a company similar to this one, knowledge of a computer program you think could help the company, or knowledge of another language. Think about what the advertisement for the job called for, then think about the qualities you have that go beyond those. That's what you mention.

"Where do you see yourself in five years?"
Again, it would be easy to think there's a "right" answer to this question that the company wants to hear, but the truth is still the best way to go here. If you think they want you to say "In this same job", they could think that shows a lack of ambition on your part; if you say "A supervisory position with this company", they could think you don't really care about this job, and only want to use it to get a promotion. If you tell them what you really have in mind, you'll say it in a way that they won't doubt your sincerity – even if the answer is "I don't know."

"Name three ways you would solve this problem."
Many employers ask questions that try to assess your knowledge of the field the company works in, so be prepared to answer these questions with your best insights. This may require brushing up on some classes you took in college, or being familiar with the company's current challenges. Some companies will have a separate assessment component to the interview, which includes a more formal test of what you know. If that's the case, they usually let you know that ahead of time, so you can prepare for it.

"What would you do if…"
Many employers also include questions that explore the moral and ethical standards of the employee, as the employer wants to know if the applicant's loyalties lie with their peers, the company, or themselves. Don't hesitate to take a moment in the interview to think deeply about any complex situation they present. You want to provide a clear answer, even if it takes a moment to build that answer.

"What questions do you have for us?"
Unlike the college interview, your goal here is to get a better sense of how you can contribute to the company. By asking questions based on your Internet search, you're trying to understand just where the company is heading in the future. In fact, it's perfectly fair to start by saying "You asked me where I would be five years from now. Where will this company be five years from now?" By focusing on the com-

pany's goals and needs, you're showing you're interested in supporting the company, all while learning if these goals and needs are compatible with what you can, and want to, give to the company.

It's also important not to use this opportunity to ask about starting salary or wages. These issues are certainly important, but this is seen by almost all companies to be rude, and a little pushy. The purpose of the first interview is to see if you're the right person to hire. You show those by talking about the best interest of the company, not about money.

It's also not wise to ask about other candidates for the job. Something as basic as "How many other people are being interviewed for this job?" can make the interviewer wonder how secure you are in your own abilities – and besides, what information can an answer to that question give you that will really help you know if this is the company for you?

It is fair at the very end of the interview to ask when you'll be contacted with the results of the interview. Once you have that information, thank the interviewer(s), and be sure to submit a follow-up thank you the next day, either to the interviewer, or to the company's human resources department, whichever you might have contact information for.

If you're being interviewed by a group, there's a good chance each member will be assigned one question to ask you. A hard copy of these questions might be given to you in advance, or when you first come into the interview setting. Some candidates are tempted to write down the names of each member of the interview team, so they can refer to them by name when answering that person's question. If that's something that comes naturally to you, do that, but you don't want to be in a position where you remember some interviewers' names, and not everyone's. Proceed with caution.

The Second Job Interview

Some entry-level jobs will include two rounds of interviews – the first interview with human resources or a screening team, and a second interview with either representatives of the team you'll be working with, or your potential boss. In either case, applicants are often surprised that the contents of the two interviews are usually very similar, if not identical. Many companies do this on purpose, to make sure you provide similar answers to similar questions, or to see if you have the patience to answer the same set of questions twice without losing your mind.

It's also common that the second interview may ask more specific questions about your background or training. Preparing for the second interview with a review of your résumé and cover letter, as well as the company's Web presence, should put you in good shape to answer any question that may come along. One of the goals of the second interview is to make sure you're providing consistent information, but a larger one is to see if you'll be a good fit with those you'll be working with on regular basis. Just be yourself, and you'll be fine – but be sure to remember everyone you interview with in this round, since you'll likely be working with them if you get the job.

Job Offer

The best way to be ready to discuss a job offer is to make a list of the things you would need to know before you would feel confident in accepting or rejecting the offer. This can include:

Salary
How much will you be paid? Is this an hourly wage, or a contractual wage? How often do you get paid?

Benefits
Does the job include health insurance? Sick days? Retirement plans? Paid vacation? Reimbursement for uniforms or work-related items? If the work involves heavy travel, is there reimbursement for mileage?

Evaluation
How often will you be reviewed? How are the results of those reviews shared with you? Is there an initial probationary period for review where the standards are different for review? If so, how long is that period?

Notice
How much notice would you be given if the company decided to let you go? If you take another job, how much notice do you have to give?

Job offers come in all kinds of ways, from a verbal agreement that's sealed with a handshake, to a formal offer that spells out everything you could possibly want to know. You won't have any control over when or how you'll be offered a job, so it's important that you'll be ready at any time to talk about conditions of employment. As you do so, keep in mind that the person extending the job offer may not know the answers to all of your questions. They may refer you to human resources for the answers; whether they do or not, be sure to feel comfortable with the answers you have before making a commitment you would have to rescind in a day or two, once you get more answers. That wouldn't be fair to you, or to the company.

More Resources

For a list of additional resources visit:
http://www.thebestschools.org/savvy-students/chapter-resources/

Your First Day on the Job

The Big Picture

New employees are often eager to begin the work they've been hired to do, only to discover that their first day on the job is filled with paperwork and training exercises that prepare them to do what they might consider their "real" work. While these activities may seem minor, the attitude the new employee shows in completing this work – and, more important, the warmth they extend to the colleagues the new employee meets while completing these introductory tasks – send important messages to the colleagues they'll be working with for a long time, as well as to the boss that saw such promise in the new employee's resume and interview.

Other simple steps in the fifirst day (and days) on the job can help the employee convey a positive attitude toward work, and put them in a position where they can contribute the most to the company's future, while advancing their personal and professional goals at the same time. Some of these steps may seem minor, but when added together, they make up a large part of the work ethic and vision that can make all the difference in making sure the employee enjoys a fulfilling career, no matter where they may be working.

The information you give a company on your resume, and the way you present yourself in your interview, gives the company that hired you an impression of the kind of person you are, the skills and attitudes you'll bring to your work, and the qualities you'll show when working with others to help the company meet their goals.

This is why it's so important in these first few steps to follow the well-known advice, Be Yourself. The person you show the company in the interview is the person they'll need you to be every day you're on the job, and that's even more true in your first day on the job, when you'll begin to build the relationships with your co-workers and demonstrate the attitude towards your work that will let the company decide if they've made the right decision in hiring you. Since the newness of the job might make it more challenging to be yourself, let's talk about what you might expect on the first day, and how you can prepare to respond to it.

Many "First" Days

A college graduate was very excited to accept his first real job after college. In talking with his family and friends, it was clear he was looking forward to applying the strong research and analysis skills he had learned in college, so he could help the company produce better products that would improve the quality of living for many people. It was easy to tell from the sound of his voice that he couldn't wait to get started.

Based on what he had told his parents, they were surprised when they called him at the end of his first day on the job to discover he hadn't done any research that day – in fact, he hadn't even set foot in the building where he was supposed to work. He has spent all of the first day on the job in a meeting room at the company's headquarters, completing forms related to direct deposit of his paycheck, enrollment into the company's healthcare program, and certification to engage in research on the company's behalf. His parents were more surprised to discover this paperwork was going to take an additional two days to finish.

Two days later, their expectations were shattered once again when their son explained that, while he did actually report to the building where he would work, he spent the better part of that day passing safety checks, taking exams to measure his knowledge of certain research procedures, and having the picture taken for his ID badge. In fact, two full weeks of this training went by before their son was allowed to begin to conduct the research he had been hired to do.

The big day finally came, and his parents called their son one more time, asking him how his first real day of work went. "Fine" he said, "they gave me a tour of the lab where I was going to be working. That took all morning, and then they had a party at lunch to welcome all the new employees, and let us go home early!"

This college graduate's story may be different from those of others, but it's fair to say that everything he experienced is part of the beginning of a new experience for every person holding a new job. From filling out forms to taking tests to getting to know your fellow workers, it's easy to get the feeling that there is actually more than just one first day on the job, since the first few days (or weeks) can involve activities that aren't part of business as usual in that position.

At the same time, it is important to remember that there is one constant in the first few days of a job that lead to the first day on the job that feels typical – and that's the new employee. Just as your résumé and interview gave the company a certain perspective on who you are and what you'll bring to the company, so will the way you fill out the forms, watch the required safety films, and get to know those you'll be working with.

The key to implementing the following tips for the first day on the job is to understand that there are likely to be many first days on the job, each one leading to the normal day of business you're looking forward to, each one an opportunity to build strong relationships with colleagues and to show commitment to the goals of the company.

Arrive early, and plan to stay late

There isn't a boss anywhere that isn't impressed by the commitment an employee shows to their work, and in almost every case, a big way to measure that commitment is to measure the amount of time the employee is devoting to their work. This isn't to say that you have to do more work for free; it does mean it's important to show an interest in coming well-prepared to your work, and ready to bring it to a thoughtful conclusion – and it's hard to show that if you're running in just in time to beat the morning bell, or if you're the first person out the door at quitting time.

It's wise to schedule your arrival time the same as you did for your interview for the job; come in about ten minutes before starting time. This gives you time to negotiate a weird traffic flow, get into a more detailed discussion with the co-worker you always say hello to, or take a peek at the emails waiting for you, so you can organize the day ahead. Yes, you could do all of this on company time, and no, it's unlikely your boss would ever say anything. But you didn't get hired because the boss saw the same thing in you she saw in everyone else; you got hired because you showed something extra. Now is the time to keep showing that something extra, since it will likely lead to positive reviews, greater job security, and the attention of your supervisors, when it's time to promote some people up to the next level.

The same is true with quitting time. Your contract may specify the number of hours you work each day, or the time when you stop working, but there are many businesses that just have culture where everyone stays for another 30 minutes. You may not want to do that, but you're not going to be in a position to make a good decision about whether to do it or not if you're not around to know it happens. The best way to do that is to build in some extra time in your first few days, up to two weeks. Once you get a sense of the ebb and flow of the end of the day, you'll be in a position to make an informed decision. If everyone goes home at the end of your contractual time every day for two weeks, you know you're in good shape joining them in doing the same thing.

Bring a lunch

Despite everyone's best efforts, most companies just don't mention lunch hour or lunch options to new employees, and there's nothing more crucial to getting along in a company climate than understanding its eating patterns. By bringing a lunch that contains non-perishable items (an apple, fresh vegetables, crackers, a small can of self-opening tuna fish), you'll be prepared to join others if your new workplace eats in, and doesn't have easy access to a refrigerator or microwave. If it turns out they have both, you can modify your lunch menu from there; if the culture is such that they eat out frequently, you can easily store your lunch in a brief case, join your new colleagues for lunch, and have a lunch at hand for day two.

It's also important to keep an eye on the time you take for lunch, and for any scheduled breaks you might have coming. While some companies have strict rules about when these occur, and how long they last, they occur at other companies on a more informal basis, or when there's a natural break in the work. You want to make sure your breaks aren't interfering with the productivity of other employees. Pay close attention to the break culture at work; it's a key piece of supporting your colleagues.

Use people's names

It won't be unusual to meet a lot of people in your first few days on the job who you won't see on a frequent basis, if ever again. The person in human resources who administers the required TB test may not be someone you see every day, but if they're the person who makes sure your payroll deductions for insurance and retirement are accurate, you'll want to make sure you're on good terms with her.

There's an old, faithful approach to using people's names effectively – repeat them the moment you learn them. If the TB tester says "Hi, I'm Darlene from HR", you immediately respond with "Hi, Darlene." There are some people who will discretely write down the names of every person they meet in their first few days on the job, as well as that person's title. If you are one of those people, do it; knowing people's names is a huge key to success in the workplace.

Be attentive during training

There are all kinds of training films that are shown to new employees on everything from job safety to emergency procedures to harassment avoidance. Despite everyone's best efforts, many of these films can be overly long and pretty uninteresting, since, in many cases, the behaviors they want you to learn, or avoid, are followed by using common sense.

If you get in the middle of a training film and think, "OK, I get it,, **watch out**. Most training films conclude with some kind of test you have to take at the end, and while each one usually allows you to miss a question or two, you're really calling attention to yourself in a bad way if you fail a training film – plus, you'll have to watch it again if you do. In addition, many new employees who see these films as a waste of time are prone to nod off in the middle of the training film – and if the lights come back on in the room at the wrong time, or if you're a born snorer, that won't end up well for you.

It's best to make sure you're alert during these films, no matter how mundane. The best way for most people to do this is to take notes on the film as you're watching it, by writing down what's said word for word. You most likely won't need these notes for the test, but the fast pace of the dialogue will offer a mental challenge for you if you're trying to write down every word, and that will keep you focused on the film. If you know you can achieve the same goal by doodling, proceed with caution; people who don't know you can interpret doodling as an expression of boredom, and you don't want to start a new job with a reputation as a know-it-all.

Do your homework on your benefits

The number of companies offering benefits is dwindling, so if you're fortunate enough to work for one that offers them, you're going to want to make every effort to take full advantage of each one. The challenge in doing this comes up when the way your new company gives to explaining these benefits consists of just enough time to hand out the brochures describing them, or presentations from representatives from competing benefit providers, each explaining why you should sign up with them.

Since most new employees have 30 or 60 days to enroll for all of their benefits, make the most of this time by doing two things. First, get all of the brochures available, take them home, put them all in one place, and set aside time to read them over the weekend. Do what you can to compare and contrast each plan, and use the Web resources of each provider. If you have a friend or relative who either is a financial planner or uses one, see if you can have 30 minutes of the planner's time to get their insights on the plusses and minuses of each. Towards the end of the enrollment period, it's likely you will have made a friend or two at work who seems pretty level-headed. Ask them what decisions they've made with their benefits and why; sometimes, their hindsight is your best guiding light.

The second thing you want to do is **make sure you sign up for them before the enrollment period expires**. Some new employees decide to create a budget for their first year, and simply put what they would have invested in retirement into a savings account, thinking they'll see how the first year goes of living on this salary, intending to deposit the savings into the retirement account when enrollment time comes around the following year. While that sounds like a good idea, that means the employee is living without any employer match the retirement program offers – plus, to be honest, it's very likely this employee will never sign up for the retirement plan if they don't do so right away.

Keep your employment summary at hand

There's a good chance human resources will provide you with some kind of employment summary on your first day, or within your first couple of days. This summary is different than a contract, and the contents varies from company to company, but it typically includes a statement of the value of the salary and benefits you're receiving from the company, as well as an indication of the annual cost of any deductions that will be made from your paycheck for the benefits you've signed up for.

If you're fortunate enough to work for a company that offers this summary, take it home and put it in a safe place. You'll want to compare the deductions on the summary to those on your paycheck; this may require dividing the amounts on the summary by the number of paychecks you'll get in a year, but it's worth doing the math. If the amount being taken out of your paycheck differs from the amount the summary says should be taken out, call human resources right away. If they aren't taking enough out, they'll want that money in one lump sum further down the road, often when you least expect it; if they're taking out too much, you'll want that money back right away. It's a good idea to keep an eye on every pay stub you receive, but that's really the case with the first three or four.

Be warm, welcoming, and a little wary of those who welcome you

You're going to go out of your way to meet lots of people on your first days of work, and there will be a number of people who will be welcoming you as well. Of these people who reach out to you, some will do so as part of their job, and others will do so because you'll be working directly with them on a regular basis. There will also be others from other departments who welcome you, and they won't be working with you all that often – but they will be very glad to meet you, and welcome you to the company.

While a good many of these thoughtful people are simply being nice, there's a good possibility you may need to keep your eye out for one or two of these "welcomers from nowhere." Despite a company's best intentions, there can always be an employee or two who feels unappreciated in their work or not in agreement with the goals and direction of the company. Rather than discuss these issues with their bosses or find somewhere else to work, these individuals can resort to gossip circles that go beyond the usual casual conversation of the workplace, creating a tone that goes against the best interest of the company and most of its employees. Too often, these employees are looking to widen their circle of influence, and they see new employees as their best possible recruits.

It isn't always easy to tell everyone's intentions the first day you meet them – not everyone is as obvious with their intentions as Draco

Malfoy. On the other hand, keeping everyone at an arm's length is no way to start a new job, and no way to live. Be gracious in extending yourself to everyone you meet, but be sure to keep an eye out for the tone of the workplace, and who is contributing to which side of that tone.

Engage in the Five Questions Assessment

Whether you spend your first day filling out forms, watching training videos, or doing the work you were hired to do and love, it's important to take some time on the ride home and ask yourself these five important questions:

- What went well today?
- What could have gone better today?
- What did I do to advance the goals of the company today?
- What did I do to advance my goals today?
- What am I looking forward to doing at work tomorrow?

It's too easy for young employees to think their work isn't contributing to the progress of the company, or helping them reach their personal goals. This is especially true if part of a new job involves supporting the work of someone else as an assistant, an essential role that can sometimes include making coffee, screening phone calls, running personal errands, or doing the work your boss doesn't want to do that you aren't that crazy about, either.

The best way to avoid feeling burned out or in a rut is to keep the big picture in mind. That's why it's so important to use the Five Question Assessment the first day of work, and every day after that. Keeping the big picture in mind keeps the small things in perspective, gives you the chance to evaluate the progress you're making in both your personal and professional life, and gives you a foundation to build on in either supporting your workplace as much as you can, or making plans to pursue a new path somewhere else. Either way, the exercise helps keep your outlook fresh and your contributions strong.

More Resources

For a list of additional resources visit:
http://www.thebestschools.org/savvy-students/chapter-resources/